WHAT WOMEN WA

WHAT WOMEN WANT

Edited by

Bernadette Vallely

A *Virago* Book

First published by Virago Press 1996

This collection copyright and introduction © Bernadette Vallely 1996
Copyright © for individual contributions held by each author

Copyright © for photographs kindly provided by Diana Aynaci on pp. 6, 24, 32, 47, 52, 62, 68, 80, 84, 100, 124, 129, 150, 154, 172, 178, 188.

Copyright © for illustrations are held by the following: p. 9 Fiona Key, p. 10 Lolli Aboutboul, p. 64 Colleen Guymer, p. 65 Rosa Lee, p. 117 Sabine Kurjo McNeill, p. 118 Jo Melvin, p. 136 Kathy Balme, p. 137, p. 137 Min Cooper, p. 157 Janis Goodman, p. 181 Kate Taylor

A CIP catalogue record for this book is available from the British Library

ISBN 1 86049 173 1

Set by M Rules in Lucida
Printed and bound in Great Britain by Clays Ltd, St Ives plc

Virago
A Division of
Little, Brown and Company (UK)
Brettenham House
Lancaster Place
London WC2E 7EN

The What Women Want Social Survey of Women's Views and Opinions was co-ordinated by the Women's Communications Centre, a non-profit organisation creating social change from personal visions.
If you would like to take part in the What Women Want social inquiry you can simply send a postcard answering the question 'What do you want?' to the Women's Communications Centre with your name and address indicating YES if you would like us to send you an information pack. Please keep your card to the correct size!

Women's Communications Centre
3 Albion Place
London W6 0LT

Tel. 0181 563 8601/3
email womentalk@easynet.co.uk

25 per cent of royalties will be sent directly to women's organisations in the UK, 50 per cent of this to The Fawcett Society for their Campaign for Equality and 50 per cent to the Women's Core Fund. Other monies raised have gone towards the cost of the survey, the staff and researchers, although most have worked as volunteers for which we are very grateful.

The Women's Core Fund raises income for women's organisations in the UK who need financial help to run their core costs. Over 100 organisations will eventually benefit from this fund, especially groups who cannot normally find adequate help and security from established foundations and grant-making charities. To make a donation please send cheques to:

The Women's Core Fund
c/o WCC
3 Albion Place
London W6 0LT

Fawcett is at the leading edge of campaigning for equality between women and men in Britain today. Fawcett is a national cross-party pressure group working alongside other campaign groups and women's networks. Our campaigns have focused on issues such as equal pay, fair pensions, part-time workers' rights and women into decision-making.

You can join our many supporters, both women and men, who are helping to fight for a new way of working and living together as equal partners. Find out more by writing to:

Fawcett
Fifth Floor
45 Beech Street
London EC2Y 8AD

Acknowledgements

I would like to express my enormous gratitude for the additional research, data input and analysis contributed by Ilona Cowe, Emily Crick, Tina Degadjor, Rebecca Fox, Colleen Guymer, Catherine Platt, Jenny Speller, Maggie Stockton and Sue Tibballs.

The computer information was co-ordinated by Sabine Kurjo McNeill and the artwork compiled by Colleen Guymer and Rebecca Fox. Diana Aynaci's marvellous photographs have added a unique flavour to the project in bringing women to life in their homes and workplaces.

With thanks and love for the quotations, wishes, dreams and visions of thousands of women, known and unknown, whose voices have stitched a glorious social tapestry of words for us all to hear. The feelings I have had reading the contents of these thousands of cards are of inspiration. To read the comments of so many generous and genuinely thoughtful women was a great gift, and I thank you.

Special thanks should go to Anita Roddick, staff at the Body Shop, the Body Shop Foundation and the Co-operative Bank for showing their belief in the project and its benefits to society by actively and financially supporting it. Other generous sponsors and supporters include The Fawcett Society, Golden Rose Communications, the Trades Union Congress and Blackwell Science.

We are indebted to the numerous institutions, organisations and individuals who have helped us in this social inquiry, particularly MORI, the Mass Observation Archive at University of Sussex, IPC Magazines, National Magazine House, Trend Monitor International, *Who's Who*, the Women's National Commission, Virago Press, Melanie Silgardo, the National Alliance of Women's Organisations and all those women's organisations on whose support, campaigning and professionalism we and society depend. We thank you all.

Bernadette Vallely
April 1996

Bernadette Vallely, writer, broadcaster and social activist, founded the Women's Environmental Network in 1988 and won the United Nations Global 500 Award in 1994 for her environmental campaigning. In 1994 she was also awarded *Cosmopolitan* Magazine's Young Woman Achiever in Politics Award and has been campaigning for social rights in a wide field for fifteen years. Her interests include women, environment, children and spirituality. She has written and co-authored many books including the bestselling *1001 Ways to Save the Planet* and *The Young Person's Guide to Saving the Planet*.

My greatest respect goes to the What Women Want campaign. Millions of cards have been distributed and collated. This is the largest-ever collection of women's hopes and disappointments, joys and difficulties, anger and spirit.

Women's strength and vision are constantly underrated and often ignored. But now we have the voices of women themselves – showing our depth of understanding and our immensely accurate perceptions of our complex, ever-changing society.

Now is the time to go forward to action these desires, hopes and dreams. The world needs the power of women.

Anita Roddick

The What Women Want survey seems to me to show that most women feel their views are not listened to and certainly not taken into consideration. This is a sad reflection on our society. I'm sure this book will go a long way in getting the message across.

Judi Dench

We must ensure the coming millennium is one where women and men work together, as absolute equals. To enable this to happen it's essential far more women stand for elected office – local, national or 'Europe' – or encourage another woman to do so. There are even now ten men to every woman in the House of Commons. The history of legislation turned out by our 'Mother of Parliaments' this century almost completely ignores or disdains women's true needs, with a 'trickle-down' effect holding millions of women back.

Bernadette Vallely's campaign 'What Women Want' has been absolutely ingenious in making tens of thousands of us – women and no doubt men too! – think hard. It is not only a history of our time but a very hopeful prelude to a far better world. I hope many of the women who sent in postcards will come forward to run their local communities, their country and this world.

Lesley Abdela

What I want is for the patriarchal religious leaders of this world to become like mothers. For the children of this world to recognise that God is not a man and has not a body but is the principle of compassion and therefore God is like a mother.

Sinead O'Connor

When the women of today compare their lives with those of their mothers and grandmothers, it is clear that massive social change is taking place. It is driven by women's desire to enjoy all aspects of their humanity. Women want to love their families and have time for their children, parents, lovers and friends. Women also wish to use their brain and creativity, to be treated as equals at work and in public life. These reasonable aspirations are transforming the world. The old settlement was based on the assumption that women would service men and the family, and that men would run the world of work and public life. The new world will see men and women sharing responsibility as equals in the family, the world of work and public life. This will transform politics as the people who do most of the caring for others are allowed an equal voice. It is likely to make the world a better place.

Women's voices must be heeded because this change is unstoppable. We can either adjust intelligently by listening to women or there will be more conflict between men and women. It is always better to talk and include everyone in the process of change. I am conscious that many men are frightened of all this. I am certain that they will be happier people after we make this adjustment. It must be very miserable to have to rush around being an unfeeling male and never having time for the people you love! The new settlement will also allow them to enjoy all aspects of their humanity.

Clare Short, MP

We want to identify how we make equal pay for equal work of equal value a reality in the UK. Women want to have a better chance to earn a living and provide for their relations to give them the security they need and deserve. Women want politicians to recognise that family life and work will only be properly compatible when we have decent childcare available for all.

Glenys Kinnock

I would like to see women making up at least 50 per cent of Members of Parliament, since I believe their combination of vision and pragmatism would do an enormous amount to help reverse the current cynicism about politics. Equally, we should be capitalising on women's management skills and organisational abilities by enabling a far higher percentage of women to occupy top positions in Britain's major 'blue chip' companies. Part of achieving this will be to change public attitudes to child-rearing, emphasising its pleasures and rewards rather than seeing it as a burden, which might help to make men more inclined to share it.

Mary Allen

Women need to have their own say, their own choices, their own futures – and society needs to hear and acknowledge what these are, not what other people have decided that they should be.

Liz Bavidge

Thousands of women recently gathered in Peking to discuss issues of importance to women all over the world; they produced the Platform for Action, an 'agenda for women's empowerment'. If all governments take steps to implement this document I think we will have gone a long way to ensuring that women all over the world over get what they want.

In particular, I think that we should all strive to ensure that the human rights of women are protected; to seek an end to all violence against women; and to ensure that all women and girls have access to a good education. This will be a real investment for the women and men of the future.

Gillian Shepherd MP

Introduction

In June 1995, the largest social audit of women's opinions in the United Kingdom began. It asked women only one question: What do you want? Four million green and mauve postcards and forms were distributed around the country by hundreds of women's groups, trade unions, religious organisations, banks and shops. They have been available outside supermarkets, on trains and buses, in book shops, women and children's clothes shops, libraries and cafes. They have been placed in public areas, attached to wage slips and inserted in magazines, newsletters and in the regular mailings of nearly five hundred women's organisations around the country.

There are many myths about what women are supposed to want. In legends and tribal stories the question is shrouded by a complex weave of mystery, so desires and visions remain hidden. Countless books have pondered, thousands of therapists and analysts have conjectured. Few have actually asked women themselves.

In early 1995 a group of women, including the campaigner Sue Tibballs, Anita Roddick from the Body Shop, the computer networker Sabine Kurjo McNeill, myself and the many others acknowledged in this book, began to discuss the then forthcoming United Nations Fourth World Conference on women. Mainstream women's organisations were working hard on the conference itself but publicity and debate remained sporadic. We all wanted to present women's wants to the conference in an unusual way and it was from these initial discussions that I had the idea of carrying out a social survey of women's voices. I wanted to add my enthusiasm to a project that would encourage politicians and decision-makers to listen to women, to really hear what they had to say.

Women were invited to complete and return survey postcards to the newly formed Women's Communications Centre in Hammersmith, London. The sheer number of replies and the randomness of distribution has ensured sufficient representation from a massive cross-section of women across the UK. What an astonishing array of responses we received. And by the thousands! As I sat in Hammersmith surrounded by piles of postcards, it dawned on me that I was witnessing a crucial historical snapshot of late twentieth-century British women's concerns, fears and dreams. The cards were clearly completed with care, they had in themselves an energy of hope and excitement – I have never witnessed so many eloquent and articulate political paragraphs!

This book is the first tangible result of the individual quotations received. Selected from the tens of thousands of postcards received so far, they are broadly representative of the feelings of those who have replied. The cards are spirited, optimistic, political, an inspiration and pleasure to read. Many women's stories and lives speak through the enthusiasm with which women write about their wants, this collection offers a historic and social significance to all women and men today.

In the first phase of the survey, some ten thousand women replied in time for the United Nations Fourth World Conference on women, the world's largest ever conference, held in Beijing, China in 1995. Over forty thousand women and men met to agree a document called the *Platform for Action* which set out an agenda for change. It now stands as a powerful statement of women's global political and economic needs today. An interim What Women Want report was prepared for the British delegation attending the conference. It was a simple analysis that compared the replies of the first ten thousand What Women Want cards with the main recommendations of the United Nations and the reality for women in the UK today. It was a great surprise to find that the visions of ordinary British women were matched so closely to those of the United Nations. The results showed that the British Government has made significant strides in some areas of gender policy. However, when compared to the aspirations of both the United Nations and those of ordinary women it seems very far from the ideal of equality between men and women.

But in the UK at least, women have come a long

way in making their case known. This book is significant in giving women their say, just as half a century ago hundreds of British citizens took part in a major work of social research sponsored by the government called the Mass Observation Project. From 1945 volunteers have been encouraged to write about their lives and feelings. The results were first used to guide policy makers in control of the war effort to gain a greater understanding of what people really thought of their lives. The letters, postcards and diaries collected are now of major historical significance. This tremendous social observation study shows how women then viewed their lives in relation to work, men and relationships, war and peace. The women clearly wanted to work, to be good mothers, to enjoy themselves and do less housework – washing-machines do appear to have liberated many women! But our priorities are different now and we might seem to take a lot for granted. Much has changed, especially for women in work – during 1945 the predominant issue was whether women ought to work at all! The main concerns during war were food, safety of the men away at war and of children at home. Debates were held over whether women should be allowed in pubs and whether married women should be allowed to work. But we notice some remarkable similarities with the What Women Want survey, for example, comments such as 'I want our education system overhauled' or 'no woman should feel marriage is going to drive her into domesticity'.

So what do women say in 1995? There are, of course, no simple answers. Such a diverse and wide-ranging group of women have many differing opinions and experiences, but there are issues that arise again and again as being of central concern to women:

- In politics, industry and society, women to be seen and heard, to be represented at the top and to be given greater opportunities.
- A fair economy. Poverty and its effects on their lives and their children's; women's access to pensions and unfairness surrounding pension rights.
- A media with more women represented in sport and in top positions and less patronising and

offensive representations of them in advertising and in newspapers and television generally.

- A National Health Service with proper funding and support for positive and alternative health.
- A healthy planet and respect for our planetary resources.
- Transport: the stark difference between men's and women's perception of the problem and their actual use of transport systems; its environmental consequences.
- Education and the political support for increased facilities; a broader curriculum with an emphasis on communication and emotional literacy.
- Better communication between the sexes and 'more co-operation' with men.
- Respect. Respect in life, in career and the community, as mothers, homemakers and principal carers for the young. Respect and equality at work, including equal pay.

This book is not an 'anti-men' tirade. Broadly, women were magnanimous towards men. From our evidence so far it is clear that women do not want to battle. While the so-called battle of the sexes has been taking place, women's consciousness has been changing deeply. Part of that is to move from the 'battle of the sexes' to what women call 'compassion' and 'honesty', and to more 'talking and conflict resolution'. Most women don't want power over men. Many spoke of this as a negative way to communicate. The 'battle' will not be fought aggressively by women. They want a partnership. 'Equality' and 'respect' are the two words repeated most often in describing this co-operation. But this is also a spiritual revolution: women want society to recognise broader ideas and values.

Fascinatingly, this broad range of women are more alike than unalike. And they are radical. They have thoughtful solutions to our problems and they are thinking radically. These women talk about our planet and its future for all of us. They want people put before profit, and spiritual values before material ones. They see no power or sense in a world that continues to strip its own resources and destroy itself. They want an 'inclusive society', one that represents a broad set of opinions and takes everyone, even the most vulnerable, into account.

In redefining power, women free themselves from the role of victims on an emotional and societal level. To be positive, or even-balanced, women have to first counteract the massive negativity surrounding their gender. Many women are simply fed up with being labelled as 'victims'. As Sarah from London says, 'Stop destroying my confidence. I don't agree that the world is becoming more dangerous.'

The compilation and co-ordination of the results of such a survey is a massive task. With the help of trend analysts and a new computer programme from Blackwell Science we are able to compute the responses using a new form of database that can collate emotional words into the one hundred or so most frequently mentioned topics. All the words in 'quotation marks' used in this introduction are taken directly from this databank of responses.

But asking women what they really want in words means that we have no instant numerical evidence to offer in our conclusions. There are actually thousands of statistics out there already, and when they concern women they are mostly dealing with negative subjects. In our background research it was depressing to read study after study and number after number of women who are raped, beaten, murdered or economically disadvantaged. S.B. from Cambridge asked for 'a way of working that isn't based on a measurement, performance indicators . . . you can't measure love'. And indeed our society today is heavily governed by numbers. Economics and science are dependent on numbers and they are a profoundly masculine means of communication, measurement and evaluation. Numbers can shed light on key trends but they can also serve to hide our feelings, our goals and visions under a mask of apparent objectivity.

People are today bombarded and manipulated by public opinion polls. They are used to make politicians and corporations feel secure in 'understanding' our minds and aspirations. They are an important indicator of society's collective responses. But to make a balanced assessment we need both the qualitative (emotional) and the quantitative (numerical) together.

Freeing the Feminine

We *do* need to see the numbers and we all make many judgements about our lives based on them, but it they represent the masculine part of ourselves, whatever happened to the feminine? Women want 'strong feminine role-models' and for society to 'value feminine principles'. The results of the cards prove that a large number of women value this 'feminine instinct' and they want it acknowledged and praised; they want to revel in it.

'There is a feeling in the country that we listen too much to the experts and too little to ordinary people. Now the people with the facts tend to sound sharper, but the people with the instincts are often wiser. We ought to pay attention to instincts, ours and the public's – and we're going to.'

So says John Major, UK Prime Minister, quoted in *The Times*, August 1995. Was he speaking to women in this unprecedented statement on the 'value of instinct'?

There are many interpretations of the feminine given in the postcards by women who most often called for a balance of 'both masculine and feminine values in society'. For nearly two thousand years society has collectively valued the attributes of the masculine and given it power over the feminine. The feminine has been discredited by many in power, both men and women. When women want equality they are often calling for a balance between these two parts of ourselves and society. Our society and its structures has little room for the emotions or instinctive behaviour. When was the last time you heard a politician talking about his feelings, or a dream he had the previous evening? For emotional sensitivity our society generally reads 'emotional instability'.

The feminine is often interpreted as those key features dominant in the right brain, that part of each of us (male and female) that dreams, has intuitive thoughts, emotional feelings, experiences desires, is creative and has imagination. It is also the right side of the brain that can process many kinds of information simultaneously and see problems holistically, as well as the part of ourselves that is involved in spiritual thinking. The left brain is the logical hemisphere, the place that controls speech, reading and writing, literal interpretation, and where numbers and symbols are comprehended. The left brain evaluates factual material in a 'rational way'.

The feminisation of most of progressive Europe is already happening. Countries such as Sweden, Finland, Norway, the Netherlands and Denmark have far more mature social attitudes to women and women's rights, and they all have many more women in parliament. It is an inevitable part of cultural progress that a society will strive to be fairer and more just. Barriers between men and women, people of colour or disability, and of identified sexual orientation will eventually break down because they are simply not valid in a world with significant numbers of empowered and educated citizens.

In business, the Institute of Management describe this 'feminisation of the workplace' as introducing co-operation over competition and team building instead of hierarchy. The Institute agree with management guru Charles Handy who believes that workplaces today must adapt or die because feminisation will be the norm in the workplace of tomorrow.

M.G. from Maidenhead wants 'a world where women recognise the "feminine" in themselves and other women (and men). These feminine traits and values are found equally co-existing with masculine traits and values as the basis of our institutions and ways of living and being.' And Carol from Moray calls for the 'the rediscovery of the essence of the feminine and the masculine'. Does a better future have room to reclaim these instincts and feelings? If these are feminine values, held mainly, but never exclusively, by women, then they should be examined more carefully by all. What is needed, according to psychotherapist Susie Orbach, is 'emotional literacy'. The pain that women go through in their efforts to relate to people who still think 'it is simply insane to be this emotional' is evident. Hundreds of the postcards in our survey carry the message that women are suffering and feeling unheard and unloved. Such depression and sickness creates unhappy families, workplaces and societies.

Women and Politics

The reality for women in the UK today is that *statistically* they still lag heavily behind on a wide range of economic indicators, but their conscious thoughts have considerably evolved and they are seeking a radical new agenda. Bob Worcester, Chair of MORI, makes this radicalism explicit in the Joseph Rowntree Report on Social Values, 1995. The report demonstrates that it is women who are more dissatisfied with our system of governance, who are most insistent on having their say on government policies and believe that the UK should adopt a referendum system for certain issues. Like relationships, politics prove the difference between the way women speak and how government acts on their behalf. Shelagh Diplock, director of the Fawcett Society is adamant

'that people hear intellectually about a problem but they act only when they are emotionally involved'. They won't act until they 'feel'.

In political terms UK women are grossly under-represented. Only seven out of the ninety-nine ministers in the 1995 Conservative government were women – the lowest proportion in any government in Europe. Parliament is considered by many women to be 'ineffective', 'not listening' and even 'irrelevant'. So many women want an 'overhaul' and even 'a complete reversal of present UK government policies' on so many issues that it is difficult to find any women who view Parliament and the political system positively. Women had many practical solutions to offer in order to gain an equal political voice. These included suggestions of 'an elected House of Ladies', 'more women in parliament' and a parliamentary system which structures itself to include women and families.

Global Inequality

It is clear that women in the UK do not face the levels of discrimination and hardship suffered by women in many other countries. Women globally produce half the world's food, yet constitute 70 per cent of the world's 1.3 billion absolute poor. They work two-thirds of the world's working hours, but own less than 1 per cent of the world's property. Globally, women still have only 36 per cent of the total waged employment and only one-third of the share of national income.

This century, there have been only twenty-four female heads of state or government, nine presidents and fifteen prime ministers in the entire world. Half of all these women have been elected since 1990. Worldwide, women are victimised and abused by men and the patriarchal system they live under, whether it is by physical assault or lack of opportunity. Of the world's one billion illiterates, two-thirds are women. Of the 130 million children without access to primary education, more than 80 million are girls. According to UNICEF, 1500 women are being allowed to die each day from 'maternal causes' which they claim is one of the least protested scandals of the twentieth century.

Studies carried out by several countries prove that between 20 to 50 per cent of women have been physically assaulted by their partner. At least 74 million women in the world have suffered female genital mutilation in order to ensure that they enjoy no sexual pleasure. Official figures for refugees suggest there are at least 17 million people displaced from their country as a result of war, famine and political persecution – and 80 per cent of all refugees are women and children. In 1990, Harvard economist Amartya Sen announced that 100 million women were missing from global population figures, the victims of foeticide, infanticide, selective malnourishment, denial of health care and various forms of gender violence.

The situation is bleak around the world and we should not be complacent. Women in the UK continue to suffer from discrimination and in many cases we lag pathetically behind many of the other industrially developed countries when we assess indicators and statistics commonly used.

Economic Security

Recent studies by the European Commission reveal the UK as having among the worst records in Europe; Women's average earnings for manual (hourly) work are 68.2 per cent of men's and 54.2 per cent for non-manual work. This is the widest gap between women's and men's pay anywhere in Europe. Only 3 per cent of three- and four-year-olds in the UK have full-time public nursery places. In Denmark, more than 48 per cent of children *under* three years of age attend a nursery.

More women in the UK are depressed, more are legally victimised and imprisoned for petty offences. According to the Women's National Commission there are 1.3 million lone parents in the UK, representing about 20 per cent of families, i.e. one in five families with dependent children is headed by a single parent, 90 per cent of whom are women.

The Fawcett Society reports that 85 per cent of women in the UK still do not receive the full state pension. Among pensioners, women greatly outnumber men, particularly amongst the poorest – 87 per cent of pensioners on income support are women.

Media and Image

The image of a woman in society in the late 1990s as portrayed through our media, sport and public life by those women who completed the cards is given an overwhelming thumbs down. The majority of our respondents want to *see* more women and see them in a positive light. In an analysis of one week's UK terrestrial television, women accounted for less than one-third of all the speaking roles monitored. Particular programme genres, such as news or sport, were less likely to have a balanced number of women on-screen. Analysis also revealed that most of the women appearing on television were likely to be of medium or high social status and under forty years of age. Advertising in particular comes in for much criticism. Sarah from London sums up the views of many when she calls for 'positive representation of real women within advertising and marketing'.

When I read comments from the women who

were angry about poor sports coverage for women, I did my own newspaper monitoring. On a typical Sunday in late 1995 there were 224 photographs of men in sport and only nine of women. These women want what W.P. from Nottingham concludes as 'a society less dominated by male sports that regularly dominate the media, regularly block the roads in major cities each weekend and regularly promote obscenely paid "heroes" and encourage aggressive competition'. Women generally call for 'an educational system and media communication that builds an individual's inner confidence and does not stereotype the female role/gender'.

Jokate from Bristol wants 'to sort out the problem society has with female body image, it's killing a lot of women's souls, and bodies'. Waif-like models came under criticism, as did clothing manufacturers who don't seem to be offering women clothes that fit. Food, of course, is part of the problem and many women identified their own imbalance, diet and lack of choice as primary reasons for our families' bad health. Sheila from Heywood agrees, 'I want an end to the "super model" ethos. Less emphasis on dieting and more on healthcare. An end to amateur gurus propounding magic theories on diet, exercise etc.' And one anonymous woman asked for 'no insults about my weight, especially from men with beer bellies'.

Healthy Women

Many write about health and wellbeing. The overwhelming message about women's health is one calling for 'good quality, free, holistic, non-invasive healthcare' and 'more freedom to choose alternatives such as home births and complementary medicine'. They want positive attitudes to healthcare and feel strongly that doctors should be more 'sympathetic and compassionate' to their patients. Christine from Manchester wants 'to give young children a "taste" of sign language, a day in a wheelchair etc, to take away ignorance and fears'. Michelle from London, wants a Women's National Council for Health and Environment.

I was surprised at the huge number of women who argue against the unfairness of VAT on sanitary towels and tampons and of the selling and advertising of sanitary protection products. Many mentioned the fact that VAT is not on men's razors and freely distributed condoms. Politicians take note: this is one subject rarely discussed in parliament, yet many thousands of women want reform. Governments receive at least £27 million every year in taxes from sanitary protection products and women feel they should claim it back. Numerous campaigns have alerted women to the situation but nothing has ever been done.

Food

Food comes in for particular scrutiny as many women ask for access to 'unadulterated foods' and 'the efficient use of farmland for crops rather than livestock', and even a plea from B.P. in Birmingham that 'it's about time there was a campaign against putting sugar in everything'.

Environmental Action

The majority of women expressed their want for a cleaner environment. Of the replies we received, the education system and the environment evoke the highest response from women. Statistics show over 87 per cent of women are very or quite concerned about the state our planet is in. Only one in five think the government is doing enough to protect the earth. Kira from Bristol summed up many women's words: 'I want environmental issues to be addressed on every level actively. I want action, preservation, recycling, care for the world.' But many women are taking steps themselves: up to 80 per cent of women in the UK are regularly taking positive action for their environment in 1995 according to the Department of Environment, even though their actions are constantly undermined and frustrated by poor funding and inadequate infrastructure support for recycling, waste reduction and transport planning.

A common vision is a transport system that meets women's needs. 'Less and not more cars' are called for, and an overwhelming majority want a 'safe and efficient public transport system', even 'a public transport system that is so brilliant that I am not even tempted to use my car'. Many more women than men use public transport already and most rely on it as their only means of travel. The car and road as an alternative is not an ecological option and women voice this with no uncertainty.

The majority of women want a 'reduction of pollution'. They want to know that their children will grow up in a clean and beautiful world and to feel that the future of our planet and species is safe. This involves government too. F.G. from Leicester speaks for many when she wants 'a government which really cares about the environment of the world and which cares about all our futures, not just its present'. Industries, and especially multinationals, are under pressure to 'take global environmental problems seriously' and many want a 'change in corporate philosophy' which would lead to a better society for all.

Motherhood and Child Care

Giving birth and bringing up children in a man's world is mentioned as something either deeply misunderstood or undermined by many. The moral, emotional and financial difficulties that women have to endure from bringing up children should never be underestimated.

Women repeatedly ask for 'good affordable childcare'. Susan from Leeds gives graphic reality to her situation when she explains, 'at present I pay 80 per cent of my salary on child care'. Given such difficulties, women want more respect for the jobs they do as mothers: 'Motherhood should be given the status it deserves as the most vital job in the universe' says Helen from Brighton. For those who remain childless, and a growing number are, they want fair attitudes from both sexes and an understanding and respect for their decision.

Education for All

Education is the favourite topic of the majority of women. 'Better funding' – even if it means higher taxes – is in high demand. They want more equality between schools in different geographical locations, and a more widely accepted curriculum that does not narrowly define success with reading, writing and arithmetic. Lessons for boys on emotional communication and relationships is strongly suggested. While opinion formers might think of this as radical, many women in our survey think it is crucial to successful future marriages and societal relationships.

Sex and Relationships

On sex, of course, women have a lot to say. There is no message of 'safe sex' from women: most sexually active women seem to know only too well the risks of pregnancy or disease. Often women want 'more, more more!' That absolutely includes 'more talking', 'more sweetness', 'less groping', and 'more cuddling'. Also, better sex education in schools and 'safe contraception widely available to all'.

Where Does This Leave Men?

Are they listening to what women are thinking and feeling? Calls for 'respect', 'tolerance' and 'to be treated as an individual' are heard over and over from women who are crying out for men to listen. They want more self-aware men, more 'women and men to educate boys emotionally and to constructively channel their aggression'. For many, what's needed is nothing short of what one woman describes as a 'revolution in men's attitude towards women in public and in private' to solve our differences.

It is time that men came to our negotiating table to talk and try to heal many of the major problems facing our world. Conflict resolution, emotional healing, and consciousness-raising are cited as positive steps against war and violence, rape and abuse. Are men unaware of the fear they are spreading among women and children on our streets and in our battle-zoned world? Thousands of women want safer streets and no war; 'what do wars achieve?' and 'will we never learn?' seem to sum up their angry and sad voices. Women want 'partnerships and co-operation rather than competition', not just 'lip service' on these major issues either, they want legislation to back them too.

Most women do not advocate violence or retaliation against men for what they have done. Calling for fairer legal treatment or tougher sentencing of rapists as many did, does not constitute blood-thirsty revenge. P.J.G. from Perth says 'men-hating is not going to win us anything'. The cards carry with them a message from women that they have had enough of the fighting, the rape, the abuse, the inequality. Some women are resigned to it, some are disgusted, but the majority in our survey just want an end to aggression.

Towards a New Agenda

All the women who took part in this survey are ordinary women, none among us can claim to be anything else. There was no weighting of the results for age, who you voted for, how many children you have or if you are a single mother or a political activist. All women have the right to speak and be heard. After reading the cards of tens of thousands of women I was struck by the power, the consistency and the clarity of the voices speaking out.

It is clear that these women feel undervalued and disengaged from decision making. And they have every right to feel like this. They have not been listened to. The United Nations Fourth World Conference on women has agreed a *Platform for Action* for women which must be adopted by our governments. It must be taken seriously by all the major players if we are to honour and respect

women's contribution to the future of our country and our world. By asking governments to work on our behalf and listen to our needs, we will all help that process.

And why shouldn't women want a better world? It is no longer possible to call those who want an end to war, or poverty, or homelessness, 'naive', 'emotional' or 'unrealistic'. These women have plotted a possible future for this country and for the world with a vision of partnerships and morality. They speak of their vision for mutual respect and tolerance between all individuals, 'a respect for the earth and the creatures we share it with'. This is laudable and far-sighted, humane and just. Many United Nations and international conferences have adopted agendas with the same words.

Maybe we never listen to what we really want. We too often compromise and vacillate and let politicians get away with simply not listening. Does our future have space to reclaim and recognise the instincts and feelings in this major survey? Can we work co-operatively on strategies to create a better future? These cards represent for me a tapestry based on a delicately woven world of tens of thousands of women's voices. It is harmonious and colourful. It speaks of hope, of change, of reconciliation and true partnerships between men and women. It is rooted in the here and now and is – best of all – immensely practical. It also aspires to a very different vision of the role of women and our place on the planet. As you read the What Women Want cards I challenge you the reader, man or woman, to look inside yourself and not want for yourself, your family and friends and this planet earth, what most of these women want.

Bernadette Vallely, London, 1996

WHAT DO YOU WANT?

To see men doing the shopping in their lunch hour. To see women feeling confident about computers.

Anne, Nottingham

I am a human being. Do not bend, fold, mutilate (or humiliate) me!

Linda, Lowestoft

Glasgow Rangers to win the European cup and to win titles in a row and for Celtic to be relegated.

Rona, London

24 per cent of new football fans are women. 52.7 per cent of female fans are aged 21 to 40. Women spend more on club merchandise than men.

Women's voices to be heard piercing the covers of tradition and culture which have often blurred and muffled them for so long.

A.P., Luton

The price of sanitary towels to drop. Men to take a more active role where charity/environmental issues are concerned. Public toilets to be kept clean.

Anon.

I would like to be able to stay at home and look after my daughter (10 months old) and to be recognised as a working woman who requires a wage – as found in other European countries. I have worked for the past ten years as a Registered Nurse Mental Health but I decided to forgo my career for a family life. Child benefit is no substitute. I adore being with my child but many people just see me as a mother – and not as a woman with values and brains who is nurturing our future.

Hemmie, Kent

I don't like the terms 'housewife' and 'homemaker'. I prefer to be called 'Domestic Goddess' . . . it's more descriptive. (Roseanne Barr, comedienne and actress)

Someone to speak up and try to change the ways that women are portrayed and used in advertising and the media, e.g. why in 1995 do we still allow newspapers to have 'women's pages' as though we can only read about fashion, etc? A British police force that stops treating women as 'vulnerable', i.e. stay off the streets when men commit crimes.

P. Mc.G., Aberdeen

Please refer to Penelope Leach's new book, '*Children First*'. It lays out a complete economic and political solution for the future, starting literally with children first.

Anne, Bath

Why do women have to pay so much for sanitary towels and tampons? They are a necessity for most women; we can get contraception free, why can't sanitary items be subsidised? This could be especially important with the risk of toxic shock syndrome. Some women may not change them regularly enough because of the price.

Johanna, Rochester

Feminism is the most revolutionary idea there has ever been. Equality for women demands a change in the human psyche more profound than anything Marx dreamed of. It means valuing parenthood as much as we value banking. (Polly Toynbee, journalist and broadcaster)

The goal of full employment as the number 1 priority of economic policy. Regional government. Proportional representation for all elections and quotas for women so that we get our fair share of political power.

Lynne, Portsmouth

Clean air to breathe. Smiling faces in the street. The sea to be clean enough to swim in. Freedom to roam. Peace. Respect for the Earth. A clean and happy world for my daughter to grow up in. Global love. Aah (what a beautiful dream).

Sarah, Kent

To stop being considered by men as a second sort of citizen. To have access to being appointed to the magistracy, quangos, etc., and to their workings, by much more open advertisement and meetings. To be able to walk in the evening alone without fear. To have help in caring for elderly or disabled relatives as a right, easily available, not as a major concession, means tested.

Susan, Welwyn Garden City

Once you live with the issue of women and the landscape for a while, you find that you cannot separate them from the notions of peace, spirituality, and community. As women we must learn to become leaders in society, not just for our own sake, but for the sake of all people. We must support and protect our kinship with the environment for the generations to come. (China Galland, author)

I want someone to love. I want to be loved. I want everyone to love. I want everyone to be loved. I want adventure. I want security.

Sally Sparkes, Artists' agent

Less bare breasts for no good reason and much more male nudity, full frontal, to redress the to-date imbalance and exploitation of the female body. Also erections – women and girls should see/know these, often! Women's all is frequently seen in childbirth.

Jenny, Chichester

To always be able to make the person I love smile.

H.S., London

Paternity is a must. Less emphasis on a profit for a few rather than profit for many. A willingness for men to share power with women, leading to less frustrating and stressful lives for both.

Jolanta, Ilford

It is possible that blondes also prefer gentlemen.
(Mamie Van Dore, American Singer)

Security and reassurance of safety so that I can go anywhere in the world on my own without being in fear. The right to be a woman, a traveller, alone and safe.

Rachel, Enfield

Someone to caress (me). To become more and more powerful as I become older, increase in beauty, be loved by my children and be respected for my work, die with dignity and linger in memory.

P.W.

Contraceptive pills for men.

Tina, London

To feel safe alone. Equal opportunities/pay. To be seen and heard as a person not a 'nag'; men tend to be afraid of intelligent women and put them down.

L.Y., Wirral

*Nagging is the repetition of unpalatable truths.
(Edith Summerskill, doctor and Labour politician)*

Fiona Key, artist/painter

Lolli Aboutboul, graphic designer

A decent future for our kids. More encouragement of girls to take or consider political careers. Guaranteed education places for pre-school children. Better and more crèche facilities in the workplace (Dad-friendly too). A more accesssible and 'user-friendly' legal system. Abolish the CSA and bring back maintenance agreements, etc. PS. Loved *First Sex* on Channel Four! *More Please.* FEM TV is ace!!

Jane, Clwyd

Advertising to stop sterotyping women as white, wanting children, responsible for shopping and the household and wanting to look and smell attractive to men. I only identify with being white – nothing else.

Caroline, London SW5

A rejection of the post-feminist expression that we have achieved enough . . . !!!
Women calling themselves feminists again.
- Equal representation in Government – positive action: all-women short-lists; E.M.I.L.Y.; protests, campaigns . . .
- Child care provision for all parents
- Better/equal rights for part-time workers
- Cheaper/free sanitary products
- Removal of sexist representations of women in the media . . . and much more . . .

Tracey, Bristol

Only 3 per cent of 3- and 4-year-olds have full-time public nursery places. In Denmark, more than 48 per cent of children under 3 years of age attend a nursery.

Peace – love – harmony – evolution and transformation! An emphasis on consciousness not commerce: on sharing, trading, caring, co-operating rather than exploiting, competing and domineering everything from people to nature. Let's work together and support one another for the good of all rather than the few and be united in hearts and minds in the light and love of the Divine.

Jacqueline, Hadley Highstone, Hertfordshire

An end to poverty and inequality in women's employment. An end to violence against women. Equal representation in decision making. The UK government to show a real commitment to equality (1) by strengthening its consultative processes with women's groups, e.g. the Women's National Commission; (2) by taking account of gender implications in all new legislation; (3) by applying the UN Global Platform for Action to the UK, post-Beijing.

Kim, Edinburgh

I am sick of the hypocrisy that surrounds breasts. If we are going to have Page 3 girls, I want it to be just as acceptable to breast-feed in public, and for breast cancer to be taken seriously as a disease.

Mary, London

Each year over half a million women worldwide will develop breast cancer.

One in twelve women, in the UK, will suffer from breast cancer at some time in their lives. In 30 per cent of cases heredity and diet factors are implicated; in 70 per cent of cases the cause is unknown.

I want women of all nationalities to be treated as equals to men. To stop the atrocities put up with by women and girls in places like China and India: girl children are unwanted and left in appalling orphanages in China and in India girls are mutilated and given unequal hearings by village elders.

C.E., Batley

Count women's unwaged work in the GNP and other economic statistics and national accounts. Counting and economically valuing unwaged work is a profoundly anti-racist measure – it will benefit Black and immigrant women while benefiting all women; and it will benefit Black and immigrant communities starting with women, who do most of the unwaged work. It is a way of recognising that, in addition to being the lowest-paid waged workers throughout Europe, Black and immigrant women do most of the unwaged health, welfare and environmental work in our families and communities – the work of adapting and peace-keeping, bridge-building and self-defence against racist attacks of all kinds: emotional, cultural, financial and physical.

Black Women For Wages For Housework,
London NW6

Fresh air, work muscles, to not need a car, to speak another language or two. Respect.

Claire, London E5

Police reports from India reveal that in 1990 4,835 women were burned to death in dowry-related disputes. In Bombay one death in every five of women aged 16 to 44 is attributed to 'accidental burning'.

Freedom from the tyranny of thinness which is ever present all around us – in attitudes and all visual representations of the female form. A ban on newspapers detailing women's appearances in their reports; they never do it to men.

H.D-L., Reading

Affordable nursery care for my children, enabling me to return to work. Education for all, i.e. re-introduction of sensible grants. Distribution of wealth, fairer taxes, fairer lottery.

C.M., Burton-on-Trent

No VAT on sanitary products. More state village schools and nurseries. More female GPs. A look at positive news on national TV, good things that happen. Cheaper public transport.

Claire, Corby

When a man gets up to speak, people listen, then look. When a woman gets up, people look; then, if they like what they see, they listen. (Pauline Frederick, news correspondent)

A real experience of being part of the global network – the UN to be just that – people united to help and care for each other.

Dr C.R., London E5

A health service for everyone not just those on benefits and the rich but the unbenefited low-income families. A faith to come back into our society which teaches one another. More equality: there seems to be a great divide and selfishness in our daily lives. A climate of jobs with an income allowing young people to rent before they become pregnant. Jobs – not 'going nowhere schemes'. A recognition that everyone is not academic, and use of their other skills. Banning the lottery.

Veronica, Manchester

American government to abide by the reservation/peace treaty signed in Ruby Valley, Nevada 1863 with the American Indians, instead of ignoring it and abusing these people's right. More awareness, respect and action where environment is concerned. Equal opportunities in the workplace not just for women but for minority groups as well. More support for single mothers. More aid and help for abused women, and for abused men to have just as much recognition and help. Better education in Britain for children, adults and people with learning disabilities. More support and understanding for AIDS/HIV+ victims.

Wendy, Exeter

According to the Women's National Commission there are 1.3 million lone parents in the UK, representing about 20 per cent of families i.e. one in five families with dependent children is headed by a lone parent. 90 per cent of these parents are women.

To be respected as a human being and not be killed, raped, battered and discriminated against in the house, at work, at play and at school because I am a woman. I want an economic policy that is not based on the unpaid and poorly paid labour of women. A redefinition of work. I want a redefinition of child care. I want equality that works. Most of all I want politicisation of women and their proper representation in our political and social institutions.

L.M., London SE26

An amendment to the local government superannuation scheme which limits max pension to half of final leaving salary when women want to pay in more earlier in their lives because they know they won't rise high in grade because of child-raising.

Jean, Bow, London

A healthy environment that includes respect for the other species, both animal and vegetable. There is a native Canadian saying 'En cha huna' which means 'It too has life'. We must start to recognise the value of life other than our own. Women must lead the way.

Carolyn, Canada

In 1993 over 1.5 million income support claimants were over state pension age. Of these, 80 per cent (over 1.2 million) were women.

Compulsory equal number of men and women in parliament – health education and preventative medicine promoted at an earlier age in schools – no more building on motorways or large road schemes started – use the money to subsidise efficient public transport systems.

Jean, Hove

I want the whole power infrastructure of society rearranged so that women have a truly equal say and I want those women who may end up in power not to feel so conditioned by male power that they in turn reflect male views (e.g. Margaret Thatcher). I believe that this change would lead to all the other things I want such as equal working opportunities for women and mothers in particular, recognition of the prevalence of domestic violence and laws to adequately deal with offenders, similarly with rape. I could go on for ever but I believe the change in infrastructure would lead to these.

Sarah, Duddon

The freedom to enjoy pornography without being labelled by feminists as anti-feminist, which I am not. End to war, better education, freedom of speech, legalise drugs, no censorship, tolerance between people, an end to sizeism, ageism, racism, and all other isms, an end to homelessness, an end to starvation, an end to poverty, an end to war, a more equitable society, better working conditions for people, happiness, more green spaces – better public transport, more money, less pollution, better NHS, better and more human system of justice, freedom of sexuality, the right to be who and where you want to be.

Rosanne, London

Only 3 per cent of women in the UK were members of a political party in 1993. 20 per cent of women questioned professed to have no interest at all in politics; 6.7 per cent said they were very interested, 36.5 per cent fairly interested and 36.8 per cent not very interested.

More sexual equality at work, more sharing of work in the home, more discipline for young people i.e. national service or some similar institution.

D.H., Amersham

Good and safe health care for all women – equal rights for all of humanity – bill of rights – Freedom of Information Act – an end to all nuclear testing – Sara Thornton and others in her position to be free – no more BBC repeats.

L.D., Worthing

I want to see women having pensions which allow a reasonable quality of life, and residential care provided for people with chronic and very disabling conditions, like senile dementia of the Alzheimer type, when needed.

B.B., London

Nearly three-quarters of the 3.1 million people who earn below the National Insurance threshold are women. It makes financial security, especially in the long term, an impossibility.

Recognition from men working on my house, being partly paid by me, that I am a person in my own right as well as my husband.

Leslie Perry, part-time youth and community worker

A good back massage – because women can manage just about everything else themselves.
Sarah, Lyon

Men!
Susan, West Hoathly

A Wife.
Claire, Wheatley, Oxon

Unrestricted power over our own bodies. No one else's power over our bodies.
Susan, Windsor

To be listened to in a committee meeting – seriously – and not have a man repeat what I have just said earlier as if it was his idea. *He* gets listened to!
Janet, Ware

We do as much, we eat as much, we want as much. (Sojourner Truth, abolitionist, author)

Not to be artificially divided into opposed camps such as the labels woman, man, black, white, etc. Each human is a hologram of a total universe.

S.J.E., Dorset.

I want a world where individual, basic human rights are respected; where institutions (the law, the family, religion, education, government, etc.) protect these; where children, women and men have the freedom to fulfil their unique potential, regardless of age, origin or disability.

Birgit, Cambridge

Ability to choose. Space to walk think and speak. Access for all. Peace – no war. Justice for women who kill in self-defence. Politics, education, equal opportunities in all areas of life (including the Church and politics).

Rebeqa, Portsmouth

Women produce half the world's food, yet constitute 70 per cent of the world's 1.3 billion absolute poor.

A wages/benefits structure that enables me (as a single parent) to work a slightly shorter week (say 20–25 hours), longer holidays (to cover school hols) or suitable childcare provision for holidays/after-school care and still gives me enough to live on!

Anon., Exeter

I don't want to be equal, I want to be free: in other words free to develop in a world that seeks peace with justice for women, north/south, where girls grow up with confidence and dignity.

B.A.W., Oxford

I would like to see more women in academia and more equality for women in academia. I would like to see a regulatory body in academia so sexism and inequality can be reported.

S.M.C., Middlesex

Women make up 62 per cent of the teaching workforce.

Only one in six women in secondary schools achieves head or deputy head status and 14 of the 117 chief education officers or directors of education are women.

People to have a better acceptance of breast-feeding mums – especially restaurants. Who wants to feed in the toilet?

T.W., Salisbury

I want love and peace and happiness, my dream to come true and to have people smile back at me as they ride on bikes and run through fields. I want sunshine and flowers, blue skies and survival. I want a relaxed body and calming sleep. I want sweet dreams, and harmony.

Anna, York

Heard on radio – man who rapes a man gets life, a man who rapes a woman gets, what? 5 to 10 years max. What the hell is going on? Women judges for women, rape victims. Life and castration for all rapists.

Penny, Cirencester

As Helena Kennedy QC says in her book Eve Was Framed, *'Crime is seen as an inevitable extension of normal male behaviour, whereas women offenders are thought to have breached sacred notions of what is deemed to be truly female'.*

I would like school systems for our children that are physically, psychologically and emotionally safe and help them to build confidence and self-esteem.

Sabrina Dearborn, spiritual healer and lecturer

All to be healthy – to evolve – peace – to be able to show my love without it being taken as a come-on – to be believed in – to write – people to wake up – particularly women – to travel – a child – a world without fear.

Nikki, Aldershot

Free tampons – to enjoy life in the moment – to love and trust myself – to not feel inhibited sexually – to become me without being afraid of being disapproved of. For everyone to want this too.

Nicki, Birmingham

A system of education which builds in teaching beyond facts, teaching children from an early age how to live, care and share – the school I work in does this, but it is only one space where it happens thoroughly. This might lead to more love, understanding and happiness.

Jennifer, Oxford

We must raise our boys to be emotionally responsible for others and our girls to be more emotionally responsible for ourselves. (Susie Orbach, writer, broadcaster and therapist)

Government action on breast cancer prevention and treatment – zero tolerance of violence against women – better access to higher education for 'all' women including child care – recognition of older women's contribution – I am sick of adverts featuring nubile young dopey-looking females.

Anne, Fife

£44,000 so that we can prepare the ground for an adventure playground to be built for disadvantaged children (the money for the playground has already been raised).

Sabrina, London

Boys brought up so they do not feel superior to girls or wish to be violent/aggressive towards them. Girls free and loving their physical and emotional strength and intelligence, knowing they are extraordinary for who they are. Then, they can make the rest happen!

Fiona, London

Local statistics for 5-year-olds and national ones for 7-year-olds show that girls outperform boys at English, maths and science. By GCSE level girls are outperforming boys in almost all subjects and are equalling boys' results in maths and science. Yet there are still more male than female full-time university students – 152,584 women to 171,812 men in 1993–94.

To see a real change in this country as regards what is 'good' food for everyone. How can the manufacturers get away with producing more and more junk food for children? When is the government going to legislate? Never, it seems at the moment. The best way to alleviate the Health Service problems would be to provide truthful education for all on diet. We wouldn't get ill so often.

Muriel, Worcestershire

I want the children to be top priority in *all* decision making – economic, political, spiritual, etc. Children need strong autonomous women/mothers to protect their needs, and caring, involved fathers. Employment and industry must reshape around the reason why we are social – which is to nourish the long human childhood. Priority on child care would logically care for all, the vulnerable. How about a new generation of healthy people?

Shan, London SW12

I think we should be allowed to work on building sites alongside men.

Simone, Cardiff

The Health Survey for England *found that nearly half of women in England in 1993 were either overweight or obese. The likelihood increases with age – over 60 per cent of women aged 55 to 60 were overweight or obese, twice the proportion for 16- to 24-year-olds. Nearly seven in ten women had cholesterol levels above the desired level.*

In 1993–94, nearly one in five women in the UK had no natural teeth. This is a third less than ten years previously.

To have and see women of all ethnic backgrounds represented in all areas of decision making and authority.

Sara, London

I want a non-capitalist, non-patriarchal world in which my granddaughters can choose to make a home for their family or use their gifts in any other way without loss of status. The labour of non-earning women creates no surplus value (profit).

K., Gloucestershire

Not to be treated as a second-class/inferior person. I have lost touch with so many so-called 'friends' now that I am unemployed and single, have been told that it is more important that men have jobs – they are the breadwinners!!!

R.J., West Yorkshire

If the services provided free by a housewife in the USA in 1979 had been purchased with wages at market rates, they would have cost $14,500 a year. On this basis unpaid work done in the industrialised countries contributes 25–40 per cent of GNP.

Equal opportunity in the workplace and interview stage. Legislation does not cover personal decisions. Change and socialisation in schools. Discrimination must stop at grassroots level. Amendment and change in certain usage of English language – i.e. 'man' as an umbrella term for human beings.

Sheila, Skelmersdale

Meaningful equality. However, this is a hopeless dream while patriarchy is a male power and privilege which favours men's interests at every class level throughout society.

Hazel, Sheffield

A more user-friendly public transport system. Less packaging on goods. A better further education system.

Bel, Rotherham

Of the nearly 1 billion illiterate adults in the world two-thirds are women.

Out of the 130 million children in developing countries without access to primary schooling 81 million are girls.

An end to war – the biggest form of child abuse. Freedom from 'everyday' fear. More women to realise everyday inequalities and do something about it.

J.N., Sheffield

An education system that encourages girls and young women to have confidence in their own ideas, opinions and capabilities, and likewise encourages boys and young men to acknowledge and respect these strengths.

Caroline, Bradford

To live with people who care about this planet and don't want constantly to rape it. Also no negative looks when I breast-feed in public.

J.S., Germany

Actions taken by women in the UK for environmental reasons include reducing noise levels in order not to disturb others – 81 per cent of women; saving newspapers for recycling – 52 per cent; taking glass and bottles to the bottle bank – 45 per cent; avoiding using pesticides in the garden – 59 per cent; using recycled paper at home – 48 per cent; purchasing products with environmentally friendly packaging – 37 per cent.

To live in a country where a healthy, green environment is at the forefront of politics and change and a fundamental right for all.

The next generation to grow up stronger and more varied; visible female role models reflecting reality. Finally, far more emphasis from established institutions on self growth and individual spirituality.

Sasha Finnigan, tennis coach

Equality for all; gay rights. For people to communicate more effectively i.e. really listen to each other with respect. An end to state discrimination against persons not fitting the narrow prescribed 'norm'. Free access to medical treatment for everyone. An end to arrogance on the part of governments who act without respect for cultures, beliefs, lifestyles.

Hayley Burch, multi-occupational

Acknowledgement that all persons are created equal. Performance and ability should be the yardstick, not gender.

Shirley, Tilehurst

Educate children to respect and value themselves, others and the world. Educate people, especially women, as to the power of media brainwashing. Make recycling the norm with children in a fun and educational way. The inheritance of ignorance is a dangerous thing. Children are born with a basic right to all of these. It is ignorant and greedy people who deny them. 'Elevate your minds and free your souls!'

Ms J.M., Cambridge

Every pregnant woman being given a leaflet on her maternity rights, e.g. it's her right to give birth at home and that she has the option to give birth in water, not to be told she's not 'allowed' this!!!

Jayn, Harrow

Exclusively gender-based feminist strategies are not enough; we need solidarity with other progressive voices for change. (Lynne Segal, writer)

To be given the credit women deserve.

Julie, Coventry

A stop to trading in deadly weapons, a good state education provision, with no classes larger than twenty-five children, teachers to be paid by central government, no more major trunk roads, a new section of the police force to deal specifically with traffic, without any reduction in the existing force.

Sasha, Oxford

Fun. Just one day a month with no children, no housework no cooking, no bills. Just a day to have some fun and adventure.

Luise, London SE13

To be taken seriously by male colleagues, to be valued for the contributions I can make which are different in style.

Laura, Oxford

In 1989 women working full-time enjoyed around 11 hours less free time than men working full-time. They spent 16 hours more on essential activities, such as shopping, washing and cleaning, but 5 hours less at work or travelling to and from work.

All boys to be mandatorily taught how to run a kitchen, how to use a washing machine, how to iron a shirt; how to be hygienic and conscious of the need to wash after touching raw meat, how to use a vacuum/brush; how to hold back when others are learning; how to support women in their life who have careers and . . . and . . .

D.M.M., London NW3

Domestically – not to be 'handling' my partner; not thinking of his needs at all times; not having to manipulate him but debate sensibly issues and differences. Professionally – all is well for me, but not for many others. I'd wish to see equal opportunities for all women.

M.L., Hitchin

Leopardskin accessories.

Julia, London NW5

In 1992 the average full-time working woman still spent 46 hours per week on cooking, shopping and housework, child care and personal hygiene compared to 26 hours spent by full-time working men.

Good health. Space. Freedom to breast-feed my daughter without criticism. Love. Peace of mind. A garden. Cheap public transport. An end to exploitation. Human-scale education. Decent housing for all. Jeremy Paxman, giftwrapped!

Allie, Swindon

Tighter restrictions on the sale of and access to pornography or, better still, a ban. Equal opportunities with the acknowledgement that women are different to men and tackle problems differently.

N.D., Cambridgeshire

Career breaks! I do not want children but if I did I could not take six months off work to do so. I'd like six months to travel, review my life, etc., but have no opportunity to do so without jeopardising my career.

Marie, Surbiton

The pornography industry generates an estimated $7 billion every year – more than the film and music industries combined.

All men to clean the toilet without being asked. Women should be paid for equal work at equal pay. Women shouldn't be solely responsible for the cost of reproducing the human race. Wages for housewives.

Florence, Dagenham

Everyone in touch with young people – boys as well as girls – should help them to understand that abortion is *not* a method of contraception, and teach them how to avoid conception. Parents, teachers, youth leaders all over the world need to pursue this activity.

Anon., Harpenden

A gradual cutting down in the use of cars, replaced by an all-over-Britain good cheap transport system. For teachers and all people involved with children to be given the status and conditions they deserve. For the arts to be properly nurtured as a vital component in society.

Jo, Stroud

Two-thirds to three-quarters of household work in developed regions is performed by women. In most countries observed, women spend 30 hours or more on housework each week while men spend around 10 to 15 hours per week.

Minimum packaging. Plastic recycling banks. More recycled paper packaging – less plastic. Our planet to become peaceful with no pollution.

J.B., Dunfermline

I would like Marks & Spencer's to know that I am 56 years young with a 33-inch waist and have 40-inch hips – quite normal – and that I want to buy classic slacks with a zip, waistband and pockets. I tried on fourteen pairs in M&S, Staines. Mainly I look like a clown in all of the pairs, except jeans.

E.B., Weybridge

More than anything, to see the end to the appalling practice of female genital mutilation, sometimes known euphemistically as 'circumcision'. It's incredible that this is still going on in the late twentieth century, in many parts of Africa and the Middle East.

Teresa, London W2

At least 74 million women in the world have suffered genital mutilation in order to ensure that they enjoy no sexual pleasure.

Women need adequate resources for organisations which are there to support, advise and listen: e.g. rape crisis centres throughout the UK are underfunded and urgently need the support of statutory funding bodies.

Alison Shergold, fundraiser, London Rape Crisis

No racism; respect; equal amounts of housework; equal pay; ban on children's dolls such as Barbie which have a low (Body Mass Index) and wouldn't be able to stand up.

Anjali, London SE5

I am about to have my first child and will be returning to work in December. I am appalled that I am only entitled to 90 per cent of my pay for the first six weeks, £52.50 [statutory maternity pay] for the next twelve weeks and after that *nothing*. Although I am entitled to stay off work until February 1996, I am returning to work in December, as my money will stop at the end of October. How does the government expect my husband and me to reduce our income by half, but still feed an extra mouth? I have arranged a nursery placement that will cost me nearly half my salary – my company (RAC Motoring Services) does not provide any vouchers etc., other than what they have to by law. This is no incentive for women planning to return to work.

Caroline, Bristol

I would like my peers to understand and acknowledge that motherhood may be a female right, but also that the choice to be or not be is also a right. My partner and myself chose several years ago that we wouldn't have a family – we are both career people who enjoy the luxuries of life, and children do not fit into this spectrum. As I once read, 'You should justify why you have children, not why you don't.'

Barbara, Northallerton

Research carried out for the Equal Opportunities Commission in 1986 found that the estimated cost of the introduction of three months' unpaid parental leave for each parent would increase the national wages bill by less than 0.01 per cent.

More help for students who are single parents (divorced, widowed): why try to better ourselves if we are worse off financially?

S.M.F., Hampshire

I am a 19-year old gay woman who is scared to come out because of social prejudice against gay women. How can women fight as a team worldwide when certain groups are still fighting to be accepted by other women? Until all women can come together as one, no matter what their race, religion, age or sexual orientation, then we will never be a full team that can achieve anything, we will be separate groups that achieve little.

Diane, Preston

I want the right to choose not to apply for child support from my ex-partner, to be free from humiliating interviews in locked DSS rooms with women who have no idea of my personal reasons, who treat me as another avenue to return money to government coffers and in doing so cover their own losses to the powers that be. I want the right not to have my benefit cut because of government shortfalls.

J.B., single mother

A woman without a man is like a fish without a bicycle. (Gloria Steinem, feminist and writer)

Has the Women's Equality Act been passed? When? If not, that's what I want, not only here but for women worldwide.

Daile, Maidstone

More research into the pill so we know it's safe – not just a maybe. Stricter sentencing for assault and rape, i.e. life imprisonment and the introduction of the death penalty to cope with severe cases. No more letting the under-16s off: rape is rape no matter how old you are.

Michelle, Lancashire

Three cheers for Janet Street-Porter – down with BBC's four Ms – male, middle-class, mediocre and middle-aged programmes.

Anon.

On average, worldwide, 10.5 per cent of legislators and 6.1 per cent of ministerial-level decision makers in 1994 were women.

Mental health. I want a ban on all media stories that cause distress and anguish unless (a) they give equal air time or column space to the women and children involved and (b) they tell me, the listener, what I can do about it.

Linda, London SE24

For age not to be a barrier to work in any job. Kindness and appreciation for the efforts made. For women to regain the respect of men they had before feminism.

M.A.W., Berkshire

More contact with women in Europe. Better attitudes of women towards other women. Less trivialisation of women in media. More positive discrimination for women.

Anon.

Personal experience is often cited by women as the most powerful impetus to organising, whether at a local or a national level.

I think the feminine hygiene industry holds a monopoly over women. Therefore, feminine products (e.g. tampons, pads, etc.) should be subsidised. The fertility cycle is natural and shouldn't cost me a fortune every month.

Joyce, London

As a spinster of 45 years old, feeling young, I want a clever, handsome and tender man. Not married if possible.

Magali

To be free of what society expects. I would love to be married for only six months of the year and be by myself for the other six!! I would like men to be stronger than they appear to be nowadays.

J.T., Coventry

There are 15 million menstruating women in the UK. On average women spend £27 a year each on sanitary protection: 17.5 per cent VAT on this makes £30 million of menstruation tax collected by the government every year.

My vision is for an awakening of the Divine Feminine within all people – that mystical awareness of our Oneness with all creation, and of our own inner wisdom and power. I see a future in which everyone follows their own heart rather than listening to the voice of fear.

Gill, Ambleside, Cumbria

Women to live free of violence in the home – in the street – quality affordable childcare – no discrimination on grounds of gender, race, age, sexuality, ability, religion – money spent on weapons of war to be spent instead to improve education and health.

Barbara, Wimbledon

Public awareness campaigns to increase understanding of sexual violence – developing awareness of intimidating male behaviour, suggesting ways in which they can show more consideration and responsibility.

Rape and Sexual Violence Project

Nine in ten female victims of violent crime in England and Wales know their attacker, compared to under six in ten male victims.

Rape and mugging are the cause of frustration among the youngsters. We need to eradicate the cause of unhappiness. Violence is the cause of visual impact which we need to look into. We as a society are responsible for this.

Surjit Vohra, Section 11 teacher

Decent safe cheap contraception easily available to all women.

Susannah, Newark

Unrestricted power over our own bodies. No one else's power over our bodies.

Susan, Windsor

Money from the government for rape and sexual abuse counselling centres nationally. Media portraying women with respect, not holding them responsible for rapes.

Rape and Sexual Violence project, Birmingham

An end to male violence everywhere in the world.

Charlotte, Newark

Studies carried out in several countries indicate that 25 to 50 per cent of women have been physically assaulted by a partner.

In 1987, 62 per cent of the women murdered in Canada were killed by their husbands.

In the US a woman is beaten every eighteen minutes and the main cause of injury to women of reproductive age is assault by a partner.

In Peru, 70 per cent of all crimes reported to the police are instances of husbands beating their wives.

Cleaner environment – more acceptance into male-dominated sports and leisure – equal pay/equal job opportunities – health – positive thoughts – peace.

Kay, Barming

Stop animal testing now – no more war/fighting – no more land/home develops – there is not enough countryside – no more roads – wildlife – give them a life.

E.A., Tenterden

A romantic – you know, the type who talks to you after sex. Nothing special – as long as he has pectorals, a PhD, a nice bum, a non-sexist attitude, can cook soufflés and wants a loving relationship with bone-marrow-melting sex . . . Now is that too much to ask of a billionaire?

Kathy, London

'I hate discussions of feminism that end up with who does the dishes', she said. So do I. But at the end, there are always the damned dishes. (Marilyn French. The Women's Room*)*

To be allowed to be equal but different to men: women should not have to become masculine in order to be taken seriously in the workplace because all women have to work and leave the home, some point in their lives now. Nor should their domestic skills be considered secondary to their role in the workplace. Men need to let women be whatever they want and do the dishes too.

Jacqui, Essex

In the interests of brevity I will concentrate on only one area – the right of women to determine their own fertility. On a global scale I believe all women should have easy access to affordable methods of contraception. In developed societies women should be allowed to be sterilised even if they are single, under 30 and have no children; this is a basic right of determination of one's own fertility. Currently, GPs have demeaning and patronising attitudes toward women who want to make a definite, permanent decision about their own lives.

Caitlin, Bradford

Equal opportunities in sports – equal opportunities in lessons – the right to have the same opportunities in careers – not to be branded just feminine.

Louise, Romford

Advances in women's education and lower fertility rates are closely related. In Africa and southern Asia, illiteracy rates for women are still over 50 per cent, and total fertility rates are still over five births per woman. In Latin America and the Caribbean and in eastern and south-eastern Asia, illiteracy rates among women are under 2 per cent and there are fewer than four births per woman, often much fewer.

Everybody, everywhere to have food, shelter and understanding.

Women of all nationalities to be in equal jobs for equal pay and equal respect. Less ignorance and greater activity regarding environmental and global issues.

L.D., London NW10

Nationwide crèche, nursery, school holiday and after-school facilities.

Effective and rational CSA.

Review of legal system *vis-à-vis* women (especially in relation to spouse murder).

Recognition that 'work' is not only paid work.

More family-friendly working hours for all in full-time work.

I.B.J., Haslemere

Min. 50 per cent women in Parliament. Ditto for local councils.

Women-and-child-friendly cities.

State pension at sixty.

Minimum wage (*c.* £4 per hour)

Min. 50 per cent women on TV, especially in 'serious' programmes.

Nursery places for all.

D.L., Leeds

77 per cent of UK women still do the cooking, 66 per cent the shopping, 75 per cent the cleaning and 85 per cent the laundry.

Permanent peace for my grandchildren and future generations.

Eva Bradley, member of Pinner League of Jewish Women

Adequate maternity/paternity leave (minimum 12 months), organised free activities during school holidays to take place on school premises and local parks. All primary schools to have 'watch-key' minding service. All secondary schools to have second-hand uniform shop.

Dorothy, Bolton

Much respect and a much much better deal for mothers regardless of marital status. A wide choice of affordable, non-boring holidays for single parents and kids and affordable adventure/activity camps for kids so parents get a break to be themselves (I haven't had such a thing in around 10 years).

Gina, Brighton

Motherhood to be given the status it deserves as the most vital job in the universe. A recognition of the intelligence, hard work and strong personality required to do the job well. An acknowledgement of the 'jobs' involved in bringing up children. All this in real (e.g. financial) terms.

Helen, Brighton

In 1989 births outside marriage accounted for 78 per cent of all births to women under 20 and for 38 per cent of all births to women aged between 20 and 24. The proportion for women aged between 25 and 40 was 15 per cent.

'Drop-in' centres for harassed wives and mums to have a moan to someone female who cares. To get a hug when you need one. A world where there's respect for children and no more abuse, a world where kids can be kids for longer and less pressure for them to grow up and have so many worries, too early. I want sex attackers castrated: that would work as a good deterrent too. Money for staying at home and bringing up our babies, for it to be a recognised job, it deserves a wage. For all women to get homes easily for themselves and their children.

C.M.S., Lancashire

More say in the UK for black women. Less slander for single parent women. Less ageism from society.

Angela, London

An end to propaganda against single parents and a huge expansion of workplace nurseries so that mothers can keep their places on the career ladder and so that being a single parent doesn't mean being poor for ever.

Virginia, London N1

The UK now has the lowest level of provision of publicly provided child care in the European Union.

I want the world to support women as the special people they are. I want to be able to hope for any job and know that I will have the same chances as a man. I want our political nation to represent women and their issues.

Sinead, Croydon

I am a 60-year-old, with a young mind, so I would like a potion to make me a lot younger so that it will match my mind and get rid of my wrinkles.

B.M.S., Swansea

I would like men to become husbands when they marry and not remain bachelors.

Jean, Dorking

In the UK women are in the majority amongst the old, and particularly amongst the very old. 65 per cent of women aged 75 and over were on their own in 1991, compared with 35 per cent of men of the same age.

As a 51-year-old woman I want recognition of older women. I want women to know there is life after menopause. I think that older women become invisible when they cease to be perceived as sexually attractive and when children leave home. I want emphasis on and encouragement of the possibilities and the richness of life in the 50s, 60s, 70s, 80s, 90s (100s?).

P.M.E., Middlesex

An egalitarian world in which all human beings enjoy full citizenship. A political society that considers our children and grandchildren in its vision of the future. My first degree (one year left), the Master's, then the Ph.D. To recover from child sexual abuse. To make a difference. to be loved and respected.

Sharon, Stevenage

No tax on sanitary protection. Days off for period pains.

Lynne, Purley

Elderly Japanese isolated from their children can now rent a family for lunch and a few hours' conversation. They just dial a Tokyo number and ask for a daughter, a son-in-law and two grandchildren, for example. Soon after, the family arrives and greets the elderly person emotionally. Three hours with them costs about £700 plus transport.

MEN!!! Naked, stripped and scrubbed and brought to my tent.

Veronica, Southampton

The right to work without people saying 'you are taking a man's job'. To be taken seriously as a person, not just dismissed as a mother. A better environment. Fulfilment.

Jane, Swansea

To be able to get a job – I am 52. Write a book. Live to be 94. I want my children to grow up. I'm an old mum, they need me to carry on. To have more energy. To avoid gossip and people who are unkind.

Louisa, Malvern

In spring 1994, 12 million women were 'economically active' in the UK according to the Central Statistical Office, representing just over half of all women: 27 per cent of women were working full-time, 22 per cent part-time, 4 per cent were unemployed and 47 per cent were 'economically inactive'.

I want to be able to live my lesbian lifestyle freely, openly in an environment of positive acceptance; a society of positive, visible lesbian role models.

Jayne, London N9

Better mainstream media representation in national and international sport, with better government funding. A female marine/infantry option. Not to have to be sexually attractive in the media or music business. Not to be turned away from pubs for looking the same as men.

Marcy, Southampton

Not to be subjected to discrimination. To have an effective remedy when I am treated unlawfully. To have a 'wife' i.e. someone to nurture me. To help my children grow up without gender constraints.

D.M.R., Salford

One in three women questioned by Top Sante *magazine feel let down by the feminist revolution and say that given the choice they would rather be a 'home-maker' than go out to work.*

Space just to be. Without having to be superwoman.

Vanessa, London

My husband's attitudes in private to match those he professes to hold in public. It is so frustrating, particularly as I collude with him in this.

M.J.C., Staffordshire

A better standard of education, a better understanding and care of females in conventional medicine. More women where it matters, i.e. High Court, government.

V.B., Northampton

Involvement of disabled women in all activities, strategies and policies affecting women's lives.

Patricia, London W13

My idea of a superwoman is someone who scrubs her own floors. (Bette Midler, singer and actress)

Equal access to health care. Stricter laws governing the disposal of toxic waste.

M.S., Greenock

Self-acceptance: stop dieting endlessly instead of eating healthily, taking exercise and accepting yourself. Getting on with the rest of your life and not hoping a diet is *the* answer to your problems. You don't have to be thin to win!!

Beverley, London SW16

Good, cheap child care including before- and after-school care. How can we work our way up the corporate ladder when we can't take the initial step because we can't afford child care?

Mrs R.M., Maidstone

Less than 5 per cent of employers offer help with child care for their employees.

Men to help with luggage – I travel abroad a lot and it's as if I am invisible!! I am very independent but I recognise that I do not have men's brute strength. Are men now frightened to offer liberated women any help for fear of reprisal?!

Fiona, Stirlingpeace

Freedom. Fresh air. People around to love, and to love me.

L.K., Norwich

I want society to value and cherish its young people. I want a secure income now and when I retire. I want big tax evasion (etc.) pursued with the same vigour as social security fraud.

Sue, Ashbourne

I want men who say they'll phone on Thursday, to phone on Thursday. Since there's no chance of that, I'll settle for something less ambitious – equality at home and at work, safety on the streets, and world peace.

Zoë, London

I don't need a man to justify my existence. The most profound relationship we'll ever have is the one with ourselves. (Shirley Maclaine, actress, writer)

I want to live in a caring world. Everything we do from smiling at a stranger or friend to voting affects the people and things around us. I want people to *care* enough to take the time to do the right thing.

Christine Anderson, Media resources officer

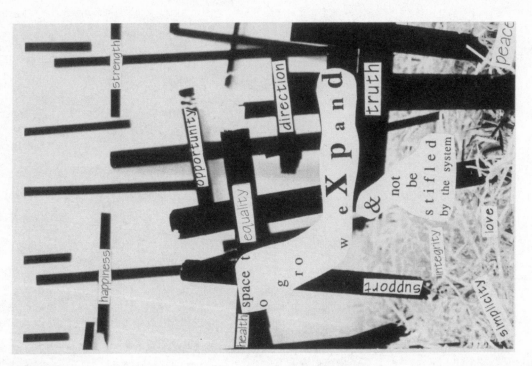

Colleen Guymer
artist/painter

EQUAL
opportunities
choice
Positive
ACTION
understand-
ing
self CONFIDEN[ce]
independance
laughter
VISION

Rosa Lee
painter/writer

'Sensuous vitality is essential to the struggle for life', says Adrienne Rich. I want us all to live in a society which recognises and honours this 'sensuous vitality' – be it pure water to drink or words to speak that are uncorrupted by slogans or tabloids or soap opera, or streets and homes where sensuality is not degraded and abused. Utopia? Yes. But people like us, in our dystopia, need to think about creating a less despairing world. Also we need to look inward as well as outward, to our dreams and to the privileged access we each have via our menstrual cycle to deepest realities. We must not lose hope. 'There is an imagination of the future, which we term hope' (J.J. Garth Wilkinson, 19th-century radical).

Penelope, Falmouth

Action on disability and racism. Action by women's aid/refuges to be disability accessible. A group for women who are spinsters (like myself) and want to reclaim spinsterhood as positive for women and defined as economically independent of the patriarchy.

T.V., Birmingham

58 per cent of divorced or separated American men say they are happier since their divorce or separation. 85 per cent of divorced or separated American women say this.

Government and EU subsidies for organic farming instead of for set-aside. Only small cars allowed in London; all cars above agreed size to park outside in designated car parks. Trolley system for cities. Complete car-free areas and serious encouragement to get people on bikes. Bus services to be regulated again.

E.E., London NW1

Measures that will effectively reduce the amount of cars, particularly in cities, i.e. through trolley transportation. Towns that promote walking and cycling in pleasant and safe ways. More parks and gardens. Programmes for learning about our environment and how to care for it.

Roberta, Portsmouth

To be taken seriously at a car dealers – whether buying a new car or taking mine in for service. Why do they always want to talk to my husband?

P.L.A. London

In 1989–91 49 per cent of women had a car driving licence compared to 80 per cent of men, and 31 per cent of women owned a car, compared to 64 per cent of men. 60 per cent of public transport users are women. In the period 1989–91 37 per cent of women made a bus journey once a week, compared to 23 per cent of men.

Peace, of course, but more. All of us need honest justice, not law but real justice, law reform I guess – but not just in the courts, in education, employment, health care, politics, everything. We need government, both national and local, that cares about and works for people, not profit. I want to live in a country where money is not the only value for everything, as it is now.

Pam Young, voluntary worker

More benefits and services for families and children should be the top priority when making decisions. Learning about child care and safety should be encouraged. I like to see things have not been animal tested or have been fairly traded. It is good because it is a signal of peace, which is good. It is also good to see people protecting the environment.

Sara

An end to all discrimination against lesbians – women-only wards, changing rooms and toilets in all public facilities – zero tolerance in society of violence against women – programmes (radio and TV) on women's issues broadcast in the evenings and weekends not in the day, as many women work.

Eve, London

Better childcare facilities for working mums. MPs who are in touch with reality when it comes to women's issues. The Catholic Church to realise it's the 1990s and accept that contraception is a fact of life.

C.P., Telford

If there's a group of people who know nothing about family life, it's male MPs. (Diane Abbott, Labour MP)

69

I want women to take a leading role in shaping the way forward.
I want a sustainable society within a sustainable world.
I want Land to be communally owned and Land Tax to be the only tax.
I want to be a Farmer.

Julie, Community Creation Trust, London

I want every woman to feel as well as be safe, able to be free to do work they enjoy and to live life to the full without fear and with confidence.

Diana, London

Unity in our diversity – acceptance and love. Decentralisation of power to regions. Complete change of structure in politics. Re-evaluation of economics, putting the needs of people first, especially the underclass and most needy. A more practical embracement of the Universal Declaration of Human Rights. Complete ban on nuclear weapons.

Hilary, Middlesex

In Asia alone, some 375 million landless female labourers perform exhausting menial chores while living with the concern that the increasing mechanisation of agriculture will deprive them of the seasonal work to which they still have access.

Bank facility for unlimited free overdraft, e.g. £25 for less than a week for when cheques etc clear at funny times. General cheaper public transport. Easier access for bicycles *everywhere*. Better part-time pay conditions.

Anon.

Excellent education and medical treatment available to all. A more holistic approach to education and medicine. More political power – a vote every five years isn't a democracy. A radical agenda against pollution.

Stephanie, London

A job/employer who recognises that my 3-year-old son cannot go to the doctor's, dentist's etc. on his own and I need time to go with him! Equality needs to recognise maternal/paternal needs.

L.J., Surrey

Six hours of military spending could pay to eradicate malaria affecting 200 million people.
US studies show that spending $1 billion on guided missile production created 9,000 jobs; the same money spent on education would create 63,000 jobs.

Protection of planet, air, environment. Animals and children in all places. Serious change in government and policies concerning *everything*: freedom of speech, freedom to demonstrate, freedom to party, safe contraception, real equal opportunities, obliteration of prejudice against sexuality, colour, gender and belief and a world with reduced testosterone levels in men.

Sarah, Portsmouth

Equal pay, men to start living in the '90s and not in the '40s. To feel safe in the streets. A better health service and separate waiting rooms in hospitals for pregnant women and women who have had miscarriages (not sitting in the same room).

Tracy, Peterborough

A culture that doesn't create psychological problems for most people, especially women. To address what sort of future we are creating (conflict/peace). Personal happiness and friendship and confidence.

Joanna, Cambridge

Women across the world are twice as likely to suffer mental illness than men.

Women's biggest enemies are themselves. I have noticed my friends putting on the 'little girl act' in the company of men, goggling their eyes at them in a stupid way and pretending that they don't know anything, e.g. like spelling words wrong deliberately. Until this idiotic attitude stops, men are still going to treat women as morons.

Sheila, Chelmsford

Not to have our lives controlled by men: husbands, employers, politicians.

D.R., Crowthorne

To be appreciated for the intelligent sex that we are.
More women in top jobs.
To go round the world.
Start a new career now.
My four children are at school to do a parachute jump for cancer research.

Lynn, Kent

The thing women have got to learn is that nobody gives you power. You just take it. (Roseanne Barr, comedienne and actress)

I want a man to hold the door open for me.

Laura, Glasgow

Confidence in myself to believe in my abilities. As a woman, I feel this is discouraged. To strive for something, i.e. ambition, is not encouraged in the average female. When you do, it feels as if you have to justify it, whereas if a man is ambitious it is accepted as the norm. I'm bored with this.

Emily, London SW1

Anti-discrimination legislation with teeth – providing equal opportunities for all, regardless of race/sex/age/sexuality/religion or creed/ability, in all spheres, not the diluted version of EO the UK has today. Free education – as long as you pass the exams. State child care. Join EU Social Chapter. Open government and full freedom of information, balanced against privacy laws for the individual in their private life. Subsidised wide-ranging public transport systems. And higher taxes, if need be.

Alison, Bromley

In the year 1988–89 a total of 813 cases were brought in Great Britain under the Equal Pay Act. Of these, only 14 were successful at the hearing.

We would like the government to pass legislation banning the use of lindane which has been linked to breast cancer, until evidence is available to prove there is no direct link.

S.C. and M.S., Middlesbrough

As a black woman I want real opportunities to grow, to have a 'real' career without marginalisation. I want to be treated equally not only by men but also by 'white' sisters.

Chui, Pontefract

I would like other women to stop conditioning their children in the 'traditional' way, otherwise equality will never happen. I want women to stop colluding with men and using their sexuality to gain merit in a 'man's world'.

Lynne, Nottingham

We need to continue our agitation for change but ensure that agitation involves the demands that include all women. (Doreen Cameron, president of the National Association of Teachers of Further and Higher Education)

Men's revolution. More self-aware men! Equal opportunities for both sexes. Better support for primary health care at home. Woman-family-home-midwife-centred childbirth to include woman/home. Friendly training for midwives and good back-up at home for mothers/families. Encourage/teach and celebrate awareness and sensitivity in both sexes. Positive thoughts/passionate life and lots of love.

Betsy

I want more awareness of, appreciation of and valuing of the 'female' aspects of life, such as all the unseen and frequently dismissed forms of intelligence, e.g. intuition, dreams, menstrual creativity etc . . .

Gina, Bristol

Peace and harmony in a world of co-operation where there is respect for the natural environment and a way of walking lightly so we live as harmlessly as possible honouring all living beings and the Earth from a basis of love that will provide abundance for all. From this basis everything round the edge of this card will come to be. Many blessings.

Elizabeth, Wales

A Goddess is an ordinary woman who is not afraid. (Rickie Moore, writer)

76

I would like to have the cost of 'child care' removed from my salary *prior* to the calculation of *tax*! (preferably after world peace).

Karen, Newcastle-upon-Tyne

1) A reappraisal of the *value* of retired people – as educators, child carers and persons who *merit* financial support from central governments (*not* as drags on the economy).

2) Acceptance that one-parent families rather than causing crime are part of the country's *support* and need sufficient funding to remove them from the poverty and misery and fear that they suffer.

3) I would like to see the nationalised utilities – gas, water, electricity (and railways) – returned to the private sector and without crippling compensation to the greedy who have bought them up.

Margaret, Surrey

To be heard when I share my female wisdom. To listen to others in wisdom and peace. To preserve my own and other souls' freedom from oppression, abuse, restraint – physical or of thought, creation and belief systems.

To be free to make mistakes, to achieve what I choose and to be quiet and alone sometimes and to be myself without judgement or categorisation imposed by others who would control me and my wildness.

Frances, Warwickshire

A part-time cleaner with five young children, who earned £42 per week, spent twenty days in prison because she could not pay a fine.

No more ads on the telly where the arrival of a girl's period is called a secret. The celebration of menstruation – and no more hiding it from men.

State-funded nursery places for all 3-year-olds. Crèche provision on the same basis as *halte garderie* in France.

M.R., London

Financial support for mothers divorced and or abandoned by husbands with kids. The CSA is a joke. In ten years of rearing our child I have received £300. He has since gone on to have two more by separate women, who also receive no money. Why should we live in stress and poverty, denying ourselves and our kids a decent life, while they walk away and have a good financial life? Why should they have more kids when they don't support their first one?

Anon.

A big change in accident compensation laws for personal injury claims. Innocent victims are harassed, blackmailed, browbeaten, and victimised by the insurance companies and their private detectives. The last thing a sick, disabled, injured person needs whilst trying to come to terms with their lives being ruined and constant pain, is to be called a liar and a cheat, to be followed and videoed constantly, to receive threats and to eventually receive pathetically inadequate compensation from the bully boys – quite legally.

Pat, Truro

Never go to bed mad. Stay up and fight. (Phyllis Diller, US commedienne)

I want more care and justice for victims and their families than for criminals and their families. No age discrimination. No fluoridation in my water – this is medication without consent. It's treating people, not water.

E.M.B., London NW6

I want more women to be at home for their children. Nurseries stifle an active mind and provide too much competition early on. Childhood is short. They don't need to rush to get somewhere too soon. Let them read books all morning and play in the park till it's dark; experience lots of things, see lots of different people (from 0–90) and have the security of feeling that everything's OK with their world. (I'm the mother of William, nearly three and George, nearly one).

Fiona, Cirencester

Some reduction or money back on containers if possible because the same product is not always required.

P.B., Basingstoke

76 per cent of women feel they have 'too many roles to perform nowadays'; 25 per cent feel stressed most of the time; 54 per cent feel 'exhausted' at least once a week and the same number have suffered from depression; 33 per cent think about death on a frequent basis. If money were no object, only 26 per cent would opt for a full-time career and 41 per cent claimed they would be a 'woman of leisure'.

Research into, and action on, male violence against women and children. Freedom from prejudice about women's roles. Recognition (and equal pay) at work. More women in decision-making positions in society.

Sally Littlejohn, software writer

The brutal murdering of female Chinese babies to cease. The raping, killing and torture of the people in Bosnia to stop. More women in parliament. Women around the world to embrace feminism.

Sarah-Bibi, Langley

New universal moral standards, not necessarily connected with religion which is generally sexist, but with God, and enhancement of the family and local community. In Manchester more focus on young teenagers and how they spend their time; more facilities and activities for them.

Julia, Stockport

To be able to walk down the street without being leered at and subjected to sexual remarks. To be treated as a person, *not* a sex object.

Gemma, Lincoln

In its January 1993 report the European Community investigative mission cited 20,000 rapes in former Yugoslavia.

To become my angel.

Clare, Ireland

What I would like to see:
- all thirty-something wars on this planet stopped – by 2000 at the latest!
- armies planting trees, reforesting deserts and cleaning rivers and seas
- arms factories converted to produce socially con- rather than destructive 'toys'
- special rates for electricity, gas, water and telephone for people on social security
- unlimited credit by banks and financing institutions with publication of purpose for credit, progress reports and accounts
- the use of 'LETS' or 'barter money' to complement national currencies

What I would like everybody to *know* about:
- 'synarchy' as a concept for true partnership – beyond patriarchy and matriarchy – resulting in social harmony between citizens and governments, women and men and people across all other separations into 'us and them'
- the 'World Wide Web', on the Internet as a source of empowerment
- the 'Tao of Sex & Love', i.e. the benefits of 'conscious ejaculation control' for preservation of life energy and thus longer life for men, deep 'energy orgasms' and satisfaction for women, spiritual satisfaction and thus enthusiasm for men.

Sabine, London

Strong trade unions to win us a better deal at work.

Every woman that works

I don't think this problem [scepticism about women's abilities] can be solved by feminism alone. It depends on the progress of mankind as a whole, and that includes both material and spiritual progress. (Zhang Jie, Chinese writer)

I want to become the best homoeopath in London.
Beverley Silliss, secretary/PA

I want to be valued for the spirit that I am and not for the package that I come in.

Alina, London NW3

To be judged for my skills and talents (not as a woman). Less pressure to have the perfect body. To have the right to fail and not be judged. Higher female self-esteem. Less female interest in men. World peace. Global self-awareness. For my daughter to experience no racial or sexual prejudice in a pure environment.

Ann-Marie O.

Low heels in fashion. Curfew on men after 20.00 hours. Higher pay for women; women-only parks. Sexism a crime on statute books and better promotion prospects.

Anon.

The New York Transit Authority has conceded that women now have the right to travel topless on the New York subway, just like men do.

In dealing with children, to know what the emotional consequences of abuse are.

Rape and Sexual Violence project, Birmingham

EQUAL PAY FOR EQUAL WORK
Women as complainants/plaintiffs in rape trials, rather than witnesses, and no use of women's sexual histories in rape trials. No statute of limitations on sexual offences. Reinstate wages councils with greater powers. I've worked in some hellish private nursing homes for between £2.00 (Coventry) and £3.50 (London) an hour.

Deborah, Ipswich

Once and for all, abolish all the discriminating questions to women in job interviews, like 'Do you want children?' (yes I do – so what?) 'Who is going to look after your child when it's sick?' (I am, I'm its mother!). Are men ever asked this kind of question in an interview? No! That's why they get all the good jobs, and that's not fair! First, because women are prevented from making a career *and* having children (we're good at both, you know!) And second, it prevents men from being responsible fathers, too!

Tanja, Humberside

41 per cent of women surveyed by MORI think that pornography harms women and should be made a criminal offence.

I would like to see fairness in the education system for mature students/single mothers. I had to pay one-third of my education costs at evening classes because although technically unemployed, the DHSS told me that because I was being paid by the state to be a mother, I couldn't claim I didn't work. Therefore someone who was unemployed and *didn't* have a child could get the evening class completely free. There is not enough set up to help women who wish to better their lot by returning to education: no good childcare facilities, etc.

Rachel, Orkney Isles

More socially aware women in positions of power. Tory female MPs have no real awareness of poverty, drugs, poor education, the traps of working-class culture, poor amenities and bad housing. They have no concept of surviving on income support, being a single parent or living from hand to mouth. They are totally unfit to make decisions for people suffering from the above societal ills. I would also like to see free sanitary protection.

Terri, Sheffield

As a survivor of childhood sexual abuse I want a society that will listen and take seriously women and children, even if what they say is unacceptable or frightening. I want the blame, the disgust, the exclusion to be laid on the shoulders of those who are responsible. The rapists, the molesters, the man next door or the brother, father. And I want women and men who condemn such behaviour to stand up and speak it.

X, Eton

According to Shelter, 51 per cent of all unmarried mothers are aged over 24.

Two-thirds of all single parents are divorced and separated women, not mothers who have never married.

Gender awareness training days (Baker days) for teachers of all stages of education, particularly primary teachers as it is here that the 'gender roles' start to be deeply laid.

Rosa, Wiltshire

Equality laws for disabled people – fully accessible environments, integrated education, grants for adaptations to existing buildings, real *public* transport. Spend less on war games and more on life . . .

Jaihn

Reintroduce the Big Ben silent minute every night at 10p.m. Ask people to pray for peace, to believe in the power of thought. We can save the world for the people, for mankind.

Alicia, Heston

One in ten adults in Britain today has one or more disabilities. And more women than men are disabled, partly because of the large number of older women who are disabled.

More cycle lanes in London. More communication between men and women. More investment in public transport. More smiling on Monday mornings.

Heather

End to male supremacy. Change in the law so that battered and abused women who kill their tormentors and torturers are set free. An end to violence against women. Peace throughout the world – no more male wars and weapons sold as toys to boys. End to exploitation of animals.

A.G., Leeds

Happiness. Health. Time for me. To be safe when I go out. Respect for the voluntary work I do.

Georgina, Surrey

Under current legislation, single women escaping violence have no statutory right to accommodation.

ULTIMATELY I WANT WORLD-WIDE MUTUAL RESPECT
AND COMPASSION FOR ALL SENTIENT BEINGS......
FOR EVERYONE TO REALLY CARE ABOUT THE QUALITY OF OTHER
PEOPLE'S LIVES. THEN WE WOULD ACHIEVE A PEACEFUL,
UNPOLLUTED, UNABUSED WORLD. WHAT MORE COULD ANYONE ASK?
AND NO I'M NOT AN AGEING HIPPY, I'M A YOUNG IDEALIST!

RACHEL, STAFFORD.

no suppression of the weak, poor, dip, ill

no greed no selfishness no cruelty of...

LOVE
SECURITY
CHILDREN

Aisha
Eastbourne

I know this is late, but I just want to say that the partial closure of the London Rape Crisis Centre is a great loss to all women. The London Borough Grants Unit has withdrawn its grant of £67,000, so the centre is struggling on, offering a reduced service on a totally voluntary basis.

I.O., London W10

World currency, international mutual respect, spiritual freedom for all. Respect, nurture and funding for female creativity on all levels. A combination of beauty and practicality in our surroundings and tools: buses, buildings, cars etc. Introduction of meditation, life-skills, emotional self-management in relationships into education at all ages. Funding of adult education and retraining centres for unemployed where confidence and self-boosting can be given. The use of traditional and practical skills rather than their neglect. Respect for elderly and valuing and care of our world nature and the spiritual worth of all things.

Caitlin, Oxford

I want to live in a society that judges women as people, not in terms of stereotypes. Words like 'harridan' and 'whore' would be consigned to history.

I want the right to grow old in dignity, not poverty. I want caring for small children to be acknowledged as one of the most important things a person can do – and it to be paid accordingly.

I never want to read that 'he' is to be understood as including 'she' ever again.

Elizabeth, Tintagel

Only one in five women believes that the government is doing a lot to protect the environment.

A piece of positive action. Secure and good education and medical availability for my child. Space to live. A world for my grandchildren's great-grandchildren. Pride.

Iona, Ashby-de-la-Zouch

I want Cambridge University (which is where I am studying) to shed, once and for all, patriarchial and misogynistic attitudes and values, for women here to be seen as equals educationally and personally and not just as pretty frills to provide extra-curricular amusement. I want this to infiltrate the employment market and women to be seen as just as good 'for the job'. I don't want to work hard to see a less able man take my job.

Jo, Cambridge

No rape! No pornography! Both of these require that women are subordinate to men. Both are injuries levelled against women by men. Both presume that women want to be hurt, humiliated, 'taken', violated. Laws need to clamp down hard on the perpetrators of these violent acts.

Debbie, Romford

Only 6 per cent of professors are women.

An end to the endless building of needless roads across the UK. The expulsion of homophobic, sexist MPs and the disposal of their homophobic, sexist bills.

Rebecca, Stafford

A gender tax – on men. Equality of power at all levels.

J.C. McF.

I want to be a man in the next life, and have a wonderful wife like me!

Kay, Oldham

RESPECT for women in all walks of life – and therefore fair and equal treatment, in private and in public: in the professions, in medicine, in social security, at whatever age. Only early education and unblinkered churches can achieve this.

E.R., Cardiff

Come, come my conservative friend, wipe the dew off your spectacles and see that the world is moving. (Elizabeth Cady Stanton, The Woman's Bible*)*

A lot more of it for those who haven't got it, or don't do it. A lot less of it for those who've got too much of it, or do too much of it.

A party who'll fight for IT, no ifs or buts. IT = respect, money, child care, work, fun, equality, housework, freedom, worries, politics. You name it.

Ellen, Newcastle upon Tyne

Restaurants, restaurants, more restaurants. Women-friendly restaurants; restaurants where one can buy a *light* meal *after* 5p.m. or 5.30p.m. Our cities and suburbs are filling up with pubs and boozers: what we need are more tea-houses. They would help civilise our society.

M.D., London W5

I want all the things listed around the card for all women throughout the world. If our work is counted in every country's national accounts it will be impossible to deny that we are doing most of the work in the world and that we are owed many times over. As a grandmother, I am owed for a lifetime of unwaged work.

Lillian, Cheshire

The sentimental cult of domestic virtues is the cheapest method at society's disposal of keeping women quiet without seriously considering their grievances or improving their condition. (Alva Myrdal and Viola Klein, authors)

Positive thoughts. Bicycle lanes. Compulsory community work for all of us. Job creation. Education – injection of funds and enthusiasm.

T.B-B., London NW3

I want to work in the male-dominated place I do without the continuous misogynistic, neanderthal, paternalistic behaviour.

Ellen, Birmingham

Make it easier for homeless people to be rehoused. At the moment you need a home to get a job, but a job to have a home. It's a circular problem!

Sonia, London NW10

In 1994, 127,290 households were accepted as priority homeless by English councils. This does not include single people or childless couples.

- End to arms manufacturing
- Investment in alternative power – i.e. non-nuclear
- End to adversarial politics
- Some sort of proportional representation
- Large investment in housing for homeless people
- Return of benefit for 16–17-year-olds
- Minimum wage
- No private health care.

Anne, Glasgow

1. More reliable, safer, cleaner public transport
2. More local shops selling organic food and basic groceries at reasonable prices.
3. Reversal of the cutbacks in the Health Service, education, local government.
4. Stiff penalties for industrial polluters, litter droppers (including dog mess) or unnecessary pollution from cars
5. Curbs on television advertising and overheated public buildings.

Ros, London E4

Freedom for my sisters in the Third World from virtual slavery in field and home, from dowry, from compulsory child-bearing, from long walks for water, from death at birth because of sex. Me – I'm lucky. Thank God.

Chloe, Oxford

In all but one of the forty-seven nations surveyed by UNICEF, women say their desired number of children is fewer than today's average – usually by at least one child.

I want a change in the collective consciousness so that those with excessive greed or desire for power over others are recognised as 'sick' and in need of therapy.

I want all babies and children to be seen as possible messiahs by the adults in their lives.

I want more public celebration with dance, music, theatre etc.

Madeline, Diss

I can speak only for myself – but what I want is the freedom to live my life as a woman without fear or shame or regret for any aspect of my femininity or my appearance as a woman; with respect from my community for my abilities, such as they are, and my willingness to put into the community what I am able to give; for the love and concern of my family and friends, all to be enjoyed without that nagging pain of knowing that so many women in so many parts of the world don't share these satisfactions. It sounds a lot to want - I think it's very little.

Claire, Harrow, Middlesex

We have the vision – now for the Power!

Jo, London N4

Research indicates that currently, by the age of 5, boys and girls already categorise their future according to their sex. Roles, behaviour and expectations learned pre-school are played out throughout life and result in inequality in post-16 education and training and in the workplace.

I want to feel secure when I walk the streets at night and know that my daughters can do the same. I want action not talk from the police and courts when thugs go around destroying private property and having sex in my garden (leaving the evidence behind!). I want my eldest girl not to be intimidated by being one of two females doing A-level computers at school. Finally, I want my wheelchair-bound daughter to have free access to buildings and not have to ask for help all the time because of steps.

Evelyn, Rugby

An end to UNSOLICITED MAIL! I'll make a donation if you print this on a poster.

Amanda, London NW1

I want people not to ACCEPT things. I want them to rebel against the cliches handed out by a corrupt and cynical press – against complacency, greed, short-term thinking, indifference. And to realise, with W.H. Auden, that we must love one another or die!

Bel, Bath

Don't compromise yourself. You are all you've got. (Janis Joplin, singer)

Women with disabilities – black and white, older and younger, with visible and invisible disabilities – want our contribution to society counted. We demand recognition of our economic contribution as unwaged workers, our civil rights and resources of all kinds to enable us to live independently and participate in all areas.

Claire Glassman (left) and Barbara Galloway (right) of WINVISIBLE: Women with Visible and Invisible Disabilities

Joy, laughter, equality, respect, love, freedom, peace, being taken seriously, the choice to grow old disgracefully, time to explore creativity. Jobs for everybody who needs and wants them; a change of government. (I want all these things for everybody, men and women.)

Abi, Leeds

Comprehensive and enforceable anti-discrimination legislation to protect disabled people. That no one should live in the abject poverty common in Britain. An end to homelessness, racism, sexism and homophobia.

Mary, Sheffield

Equality at all ages. Not to be treated as though you are suddenly dim-witted at soon as you reach 60!

Joy, London

There is a lack of emergency accommodation for homeless women – a survey found that less than one in eight bed spaces in hostels were for women.

I want
One year's maternity leave and
Up to two years' further 'homecare leave' (paid for by State/local authority in tandem) per child, as in Scandinavia.

Cathy, London N16

A society where decisions are based on the heart rather than the head.

Scilla, Sherborne, Glos.

To live in a better environment, i.e. countryside room with a good view! For my mother and me to be at peace and her to get to know me.

Debi, London SE1

An end to women being defined economically through their relationship to men. equality of child care. Action against violence against women, both physical and psychological.

S. Jones, Birmingham

According to Shelter, 15% of all families with dependent children are lone parent families and 90 per cent of lone parents are women.
Lone parents' income is generally less than half that of two-parent families.

Male employers to stop assuming that women over 30 are not worth employing because they will have babies. Media representations of women not to be so stereotyped. Men to take their share of family and domestic responsibilities.

Sue, Reigate

Access for disabled people to all public buildings now – should be legal requirement. Equal opportunities legislation which works for all disadvantaged groups. Regulation of rents on 'private' property – all rents registered by law. National campaign to educate about equal opportunities to combat right-wing concept of 'political correctness'. 'Unmarried' status of women to be recognised. State investment in housing and employment. Bill of rights – Charter 88. Violence against women should receive appropriate prison sentence.

Katharine, Leicester

I want to be able to feel comfortable with my work, my hair, my face, my nails, my breasts, stomach, thighs, butt, etc. etc. I don't want to be told how, why and when. I think cosmetic surgery should be banned: it is positively evil.

P.T., Worcestershire

In the UK, there are more than 3 million adult women with a recognised disability.

Recognition of the rights of indigenous peoples.

Tara, London SW18

More research to find safer methods of contraception (without testing on Third World women!). Obligation for employers to provide maternity/paternity leave. Decriminalisation of prostitution. An end to discrimination against prostitutes. Legal rights for prostitutes.

Maxine, Whitstable

No pornography – no Page 3, even.

Emily, London EC4

There are 300 million indigenous peoples worldwide, virtually all of whom either have no power over their lands or are threatened.

105

Equal pay – I am weary and tired of working long hours as a single parent and only earning a salary which I *know* is less than many men who aren't so skilled, and work less hours than I do.

Elaine, Birmingham

It should be compulsory for local authorities to provide adequate numbers of public lavatories. Travelling in Britain is very difficult for women alone. There are fewer and fewer public loos; those that do exist close around 5p.m. It's not easy for a woman alone to go into a pub – which is the only alternative. Sorry – this is a mundane 'wish' but one that would make a big difference to my freedom and confidence!

Bronwen, Sale

More free consumer information. More car-free town centres. More free sport especially for women. More food-processing information. More activities for the lonely and emotionally disabled.

Eva, Surrey

In the UK, there are 2.248 million recognised female incontinence sufferers.

WHAT DO YOU WANT?

I want to drive Formula 1
racing cars. I want to win
races. I want to win the
Formula 1 world championship.
Formula 1 racing cars are extremely
sensitive pieces of equipment. The race is
about understanding the car, — + plus
endurance — something women have more of -so says current
physiology
or take it to your nearest
branch of The Body Shop
by 30 August 1995

WHAT WOMEN WANT

3-4 Albion Place

Galena Road

London W6 OLT

Name SARAH,

LONDON · NW6

Would you like to know more?   Yes/No

1024

MILLIO

TEL: 071 25

LONDON N

3 - PM

199

CFC 2

36

28

I want access for all
to continuing education
leading to fulfillment and security.
I want equal access for all
to legal aid, towards
better relationships and peace
of mind.

Linda, Newcastle upon Tyne.

A spiritual and ecological imperative taking precedence over capitalist free market greed. A culture of positivism and love taking precedence over the current cult of fear and violence.

L.H. Stoke, Hartland

More direct honest communication, particularly between the sexes.
More cuddling, less groping . . .
More women in government and policy-making positions.
Less TV coverage of football. Introduction of sports channel for this purpose only?

M.A.Z., Sheffield

What I want is a rich man I only have to see a couple of times a month who will set me up in a really beautiful house. This will liberate me from having to work and empower me to spend time on shopping and having fun with my women friends.

L.T., London W8

If you obey all the rules you miss all the fun.
(Katharine Hepburn, actress)

More women's sport on TV and radio; there's a lot of it about, only the men get the coverage!

Roz, Cambridge

Good-quality, affordable child care: at present I pay 80 per cent of my income on child care. I would also like to be paid the going rate for my job; in spite of having worked for ten years I am paid 70 per cent of the appropriate salary for the job.

Susan, Leeds

A Minister for Women cabinet post and associated government machinery.

Sandra, Aberdeen

Britain has the widest gap between women's and men's pay anywhere in Europe.

Independent taxation and entitlement to benefits, regardless of marital and cohabitation status; an end to the nuclear family as the 'best' way to rear children; a basic income for everyone; positive action in employment and education for disabled groups; housing for all!! Do away with Child Support Act!!

J.B., Bristol

True equality with men, especially job opportunities; equal pay, equal respect; an end to all the media hype about attractive females being slim and delicate; there are a lot of us big strong women, with muscles, even!

Sheila, Cumbria

I want Tampax to be free! I want realistic-looking women in the media.

Jo, Wiltshire

Women aged 65–69 have an average income from occupational pensions of just £7 per week compared to £33 per week for men of the same age.

Stop child abuse.
Honest landlords and car mechanics (who don't rip you off if you're female).
Stop incest and family abuse.
More men with vulnerable feelings.
Positive thinking worldwide.
Acceptance of women in the workplace.
To sort out the problem society has with female body image: it's killing a lot of women's souls (and bodies).

Jokate, Bristol

Peace of mind
No hassles
A variety of entertainment
A man now and again, not permanent
Like to be slimmer
Enough money to enjoy life without being short
A man who doesn't moan, and keeps his mouth shut and his wallet open

Mrs N.

Action on computer porn.
Action on paedophiles who travel abroad to abuse vulnerable children in Third World countries.
International and nationally co-ordinated actions.
Safe, frequent late-night public transport.

Jeanne, Lancashire

The British size range for clothes was set in the early 1950s. The average shape of British women has changed considerably since then – today's woman has bigger and lower breasts, a thicker waist, larger upper hips, a more rounded tummy, fuller upper arms and a bigger ribcage. But the majority of clothing manufacturers still base the patterns for today's clothes on the 1950s measurements.

I want the diet industry to stop the propaganda; real democracy; paternity leave; access for all; enlightened men; a clean environment and car-free streets; better human rights abroad and in Britain; proportional representation; peace; action on racism and anti-Semitism.

Sarah, Kettering, Northamptonshire

Less fighting and more negotiation, which means less politics; rather a desire to truly live more in peace and harmony (worldwide) instead of being motivated by greed, power and nationalist interest.

Anita, London

1. A women's movement that embraces all the issues that affect women worldwide: development, violence (state and interpersonal), class, sexuality, ethnicity, workplace, family life, mothering fertility, education, war, poverty. 2. A movement that thinks, talks, listens, acts and has pride in love, respect, diversity. 3. A movement that can communicate within itself and with those outside. 4. A movement that welcomes everyone.

Kirsten, London

I myself have never been able to find out precisely what feminism is: I know that people call me a feminist whenever I express sentiments that differentiate me from a doormat. (Rebecca West, writer)

I want the world to be more peaceful. I get scared when wars are going on.

Miranda, Kew

Each and every person should be educated from earliest childhood to be imaginative. Each person should be different from every other person. Each person should be interested in every other person (not just tolerant)!

J.L.C., Sussex

Fearless role models. All women clubbing together to become the first sex. Insistence from all women on *Top-class child care free for everyone everywhere.* And of course economic independence for women!

Win, Cardiff

No one can make you feel inferior without your own consent. (Eleanor Roosevelt, American stateswoman)

A good fella!! Yeah . . . with strength and power to get him through the night!!! One who has loadsa dosh and a nice bum. Send one soon!

Lisa, Manchester

Girls to wear trousers in comprehensive schools.

Cerys, Wales

Choices, not just for women but for men too. Traditional 'male' and 'female' ways to behave in society are too restrictive. Everyone should have the freedom to be who they want to be and express both their 'masculine' and 'feminine' qualities without fear of judgement by society.

Helen, London SW13

74 per cent of respondents in couple households said household shopping should be equally shared; 47 per cent actually do share equally.

Appreciation for being a housewife and a mum –
good ones are worth their weight in gold.
Carole, Chorleywood

A sorted self – then everything else falls into
place/becomes clearer/more manageable/isn't
such a struggle and you are then able to do more.
Lizzie, London

A fair society helping everyone to have
opportunities to use their skills and be seen as
worth their hire and in which everyone recognises
responsibility for each other. I should be so lucky!!
G.S., Oldham

*Because of their agelong training in human
relations – for that is what feminine intuition is,
really – women have a special contribution to
make to any group enterprise. (Margaret Mead,
American anthropologist)*

Sabine Kujo McNeill, computer networker

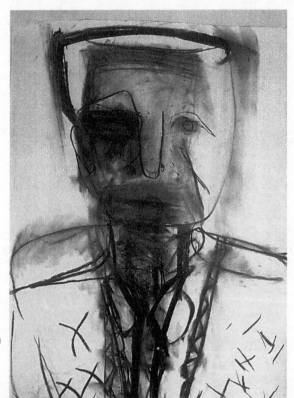

Let me listen to me and not to them
(Gertrude Stein)

Jo Melvin, artist/painter

300 women MPs.

Susan, Devon

How is it that men get the world and I get this poxy little postcard?

I want more power, more recognition that women are not a minority group, equal access, equal pay, equal opportunities; to be patronised less.

Sally, Bristol

I want more help for carers, most of whom are women, and help for those they care for, of whom I am one. I cannot choose those who are employed by the council to care for me for four hours a week. I want choice in this matter and more help.

S.T., London NW3

Thirty-three carefully selected housebound elderly people in Chicago run a telephone advice line for children from 3p.m. to 6p.m. daily. Up to 500 calls per month are handled, covering subjects from bullying at school to teenage pregnancy.

Less noise (roads, pop music). Less speed obsession. Less sport. Less 'news' dominance. More tranquility. Women having female fun with other women.

Sandra, Netherlands

More women in political power to create a new governing process that focuses on educational welfare and cultural progress and ends war, violence and the excessive competitive greed for money, property and territories.

Janice, London W4

The views and opinions of middle-aged and older women from all races to be sought, heard and valued and reported. Educating girls at the earliest age not to conform, not to feel they have only the choice of marriage and motherhood.

Vivien, Pinner

In one week's analysis of UK terrestrial television, women accounted for under one-third of all the speaking roles monitored. Particular programme genres (such as the news and sport) were less likely than others to have a balanced number of women on-screen. Analysis also revealed that most of the women appearing on television were likely to be of medium or high social status and under 40 years of age.

No wars – keep the toys from the boys. An international awareness of destruction of war. And more comprehensive media coverage of international politics.

Not a piece of the action but a lot of positive thoughts and action.

Penny, Reading

A higher profile for women's issues in the political sphere. Not to be patronised with policies which are merely tokenism.

C.B., Leicester

A society in which the patriarchal, hierarchical, dualistic structures no longer exist. Equality and respect for difference. A holistic lifestyle in every aspect. Peace, living in harmony with all things and people.

K.W., London SW8

Betty Boothroyd became the first woman speaker of the House of Commons in 1992.

Louie Bennett was the first woman president of the Irish Trade Unions Congress in 1931, combining women's suffrage with Irish nationalism and the rights of workers. She helped found the Irishwomen's Suffrage Foundation in 1913.

I want: no racism, no pain, to feel safe, more money, peace in the world and in my life, self-confidence, independence, fun, love, a holiday in Washington, DC, honesty, freedom, to meet Clint Eastwood, children, a fulfilling career. I want to be happy.

N.W., Durham

To be safe at night – not to worry about being attacked. To be loved by someone as much as I love them. For men to say what they really feel. I want conflict, oppression and unlawful killings to stop. I want someone to sponsor me to go to drama school.

Kerensa, Plymouth

I want a world where my son can grow up without taking on the macho ideals of current society, where I can be safe to go out when and where I want, where I can work for equal pay in the knowledge that my son is in affordable, quality child care. I want to be treated as an individual and not as an object regardless of my sexuality, where my gay and lesbian friends don't have to live in fear of being attacked. I want better health care for women and better education in birth control, abortion, relationships and child care compulsory from the age of 15 in all schools. I want society to stop exploiting women to sell its multinational goods, and for the media to stop patronising women who achieve. I want women of all minorities freed to live.

Caroline, Winchester

98 per cent of women say they would like their husband or lover to talk more about his feelings, thoughts, and dreams, and to ask them more about their own.

Safe food – much lower use of pesticide, no irradiation. More public education on good food – a celebration of good food. A vibrant, creative education for our children, coupled with flexible, exciting after- and pre-school care for those parents who work. A more beautiful public environment, more public works of art by women.

Catherine, Worcestershire

Eradication of ignorance worldwide – of the rights and mistreatment at every level, in every circumstance, of women. This can only be achieved through thorough education and reassessment of values within cultures.

Alex, Donegal, Ireland

Everyone to celebrate their unique 'self' and 'be' with their power, and this is happening as I write. LOVE.

Annabel, Manchester

Proportion of women's works in national collections: 0.2 per cent, Portrait Gallery, Scotland; 9.4 per cent Tate Gallery, London; 0.4 per cent National Gallery, London; and 0.1 per cent National Gallery, Scotland.

More women in upper management. Equal pay in all areas, more opportunity for feminist employment, encouragement for and access to computer facilities and cultural representations and theory production. Support for single and women-identified women.

Tabitha Goode, photographic artist

Respect and equality internationally. Status for older women. Rights for all women and especially babies, children and older people. Sharing of domestic responsibilities to give women time to play and have creative time.

Denny, Bristol

World peace; more tolerance in all areas and issues; clean environment; more women in positions of real power; more respect for children; equal opportunities; get men to face up to and tackle the real issues – if not, leave it to us!

Sarah, Dorset

A less polluted world. Pre-school education for all. Every working adult should have access to paternity leave, compassionate leave for family emergencies of up to 20 days, bereavement leave of up to five days, full-time rights for part-time workers, career breaks of up to one year. Retirement age of 60 years.

T.A.G., Bognor Regis

While women represent 50 per cent of the world's population, they perform nearly two-thirds of all working hours, receive only 10 per cent of the world income and own less than 1 per cent of world property.

Britain's Overseas Development Authority to stop funding China's coercive population control programme which denies women across China and occupied Tibet freedom of choice and causes unimaginable suffering as a result of forced sterilisations and abortions.

Y.B., London

Liberty, justice, purity, i.e. the suffragette aims symbolised by the colours you've used on this card.
Liberty – political freedom; personal freedom.
Justice – for others, and equal opportunities for women.
Purity – a clean environment; personal health.

Mrs J., Haddenham

I would like us all to care more about the environment and for people to stop judging everything in terms of money. You can't eat pound notes or drink them, when the world runs out of grain and water, as it is doing. We waste so much of everything. For cleaner air. For politicians to stop lying to us.

Louise, Grimsby

There will never be complete equality until women themselves help to make laws and elect lawmakers. (Susan B. Anthony, American suffragette)

A world where each person has the chance to find, develop and offer their particular gift(s), whether it be networking, song writing, tree planting, parenting etc. and this individuality to be honoured – a seeking of what is unique and special in everyone, where we value life over control and profit.

Susannah, Devon

Equality for the sexes. Freedom from fanatics. World responsibility for the environment. Protection for children from mad adults. A socialist government. To travel and see the world, to be fit, healthy and happy. A good sex life! A nice stable home. No debt and a holiday. Probably what everyone else wants.

Sheila, Edinburgh

Growing and eating of organic food to be the norm, not the exception. A clean, healthy environment for all.

J.B., Norwich

The day will come when man will recognise woman as his peer, not only at the fireside, but in the councils of the nation. Then, and not until then, will there be the perfect comradeship, the ideal union between the sexes that shall result in the highest development of the race. (Susan B. Anthony, American suffragette)

I want the right to decide whether I shall be kept alive or not – in consultation with doctors: if I should suffer a dense stroke I would rather they used their efforts to save someone else.

Olive Jahn, researcher

For machismo to wither and die

Lynette, Leeds

More female doctors – and the right to choose medicines which do not harm our bodies. I am fed up with being pressured by the medical profession to use unnatural contraceptives, which have hideous side-effects. FREEDOM PLEASE!

Elspeth, Little Missenden

Sane political priorities. Why spend billions on out-dated trident missiles while closing hospitals? We need politicians who put social values and social justice first.

Martha, London SW1

Between 1948 and 1992 the UN spent $8.3 billion on peacekeeping, compared to about $30 trillion spent by the world's governments on the military.

I would like to see women's right to pursue a paid career of their choice to be sufficiently established that they are able to decide instead to work in the home and bring up their children without feeling traitors to the feminist cause.

Jill, Manchester School of Management

Abolition of breast augmentation and implants. Australia and the US have practically banned silicone implants. UK *et al.* must follow. *Implants are killing women*. Women should not be denied all the information on this subject as they are now.

Sue, Burton upon Trent

Action to be taken concerning removing women's reproductive organs without full and clear consent *and* GPs who dish out HRT like no tomorrow *and* less medical intervention in childbirth e.g. episiotomy, Caesarean and epidurals.

Tracey, Birmingham

In 1991, mothers were less likely than fathers to be employed (51 per cent v. 92 per cent), much less likely to have a full-time job (31 per cent v. 91 per cent) but much more likely to have a part-time job (20 per cent v. 21 per cent). The unemployment rate for mothers was nearly three times as high (13 per cent v. 5 per cent).

I would like to live in a world with more honesty: less style, more substance; more direct speaking in every kind of communication – especially from politicians acknowledging uncertainty and from everyone in direct friendships. And I want much more listening to happen.

Judi, University of Bath

I want a democratic socialist world at peace, giving security and equality to everyone. I want a world where children can enjoy the freedom and excitement and beauty of childhood. I want a world where everyone can be creative, without competition or constriction. (I also want a second life – but that's fantasy, not rational wishing.)

Barbara, London WC1

I want an end to the mindless patronising advertisements on television (etc.) which tell women how they should look feel and behave – especially Mr Sheen bloody ads and l'Oréal junk!

Gemma, West Yorkshire

In over fifty countries, women represent more than 50 per cent of communications students. Despite their training, in no country do women hold fifty per cent of media jobs – either in radio and television, or in the print media. Outside Europe this share frequently falls below 30 per cent.

I think that there should be a greater number of sports for women to play both at home (UK) and internationally. Why should my generation be expected to grow up and do the housework.

Arabella (aged 11), Middlesex

Worldwide: An end to domestic violence. Proper legal and support systems for women enduring domestic violence. Minimum pay legislation and equal pay for equal work. Equality of pension rights for women. Access to free child care in the workplace.

Anne, London NW5

I want women to stop being aggressive and strident and to find their role in partnership with men. I want people to realise equality is a myth, a fable, but equal opportunities is the reality.

Sam, Windsor

In 1993 there were over 800,000 incidents of domestic violence against women compared to 300,000 against men.

I would like . . . less cruelty to animals (animal testing), peace, the NHS to get much better funds, the ozone layer filled in, more help for the elderly, animals and children who are lonely and abused. More friendships that last for ever.

Katie Rodgers, aged 13

An 'animal friendly' world where our 'furry and feathered' fellow creatures are no longer eaten, experimented on or exploited for human greed.
A 'no smoking' policy.
A place where there is freedom to be ourselves.

Juliette, Colchester

A better widow's pension. Age related. It's not our fault our husbands die young
More jobs for older people (50 upwards)
Doctors who listen and who stay longer than 45 seconds on daytime home visits
Lottery money for the NHS
So-called top people to pay same penalties as anyone else (Diana and traffic wardens)
Never to allow organs to be taken without consent (they are thinking of this)

Rose, Blackpool

An absolute bar on any substance derived from aborted foetuses or their placenta for either medical or cosmetic use.
A bar on 'newspeak', i.e. the use of words to conceal the real meaning.

J.M.P., Bolton

Among pensioners women greatly outnumber men, particularly amongst the poorest – 87 per cent of pensioners on income support are women.

CLOTHES and relationships

COWBOY BOOTS

CHAINSTORE TROUSERS

PANTS EVEN JOHN THE BAPTIST WOULDN'T WEAR

Well - it starts with dressing to please on the first date - for instance - you're prepared to look like a battenberg cake because he'd once mentioned he liked yellow.

VARIOUS SHADES OF YELLOW

He might start to wear something that echoed your outfit - to show you're the same TYPE.

DOC MARTIN JIVE-O-DINEY TYPE

CRINKLY LINEN ARTY TYPE

It is highly likely that at some early stage one of the pair will start buying clothes for the other – WOMEN generally buy for men on matters of STYLE and TASTE, MEN buy for women on matters of SEX.

I THOUGHT YOU NEEDED A NEW SWEATER

I THOUGHT YOU NEEDED A NEW BASQUE

There are some couples who wear identical outfits or matching patches on jeans; SWEET? I don't think so.

People can always look good to their partners - love is blind to adornment... others just must have an A-level in Dressing.

Cathy Balme, cartoonist

Min Cooper, illustrator

Capital punishment to be introduced for the crimes of rape, sexual abuse, physical abuse and mental abuse!

P.O., Luton

What women want is better communication between them and men. Negotiation instead of competition. A peaceful world for children to grow up into.

Elisabeth, Leeds

Equal rights for retired women's pensions. Sex discrimination against women: men receive their invalidity pension, also injury benefit, up to 70 years, but women's pensions cease at the age 65. I myself will lose £70 a week, a disgrace!

Joan, Co. Durham

Analysis of income data from the 1991 census showed that 76 per cent of people in the lowest tenth were women whilst 83 per cent of those in the highest tenth were men.

I do not believe, as do radical feminists, that women should ever be on the same level as men, for the two sexes are too different in my mind. Neither should dominate all areas, but rather I want us each to use our personal talents to concentrate on relevant areas in life. I want women to believe they can reach an important position in their life and not be overtaken by men each time due to our highly sexist system. I thus call for changes in the large institutions – let us get to the root of the problem.

Rachel, Newquay

Equality in racing, e.g. women drivers in Formula One racing.

Melanie, Lincolnshire

All those men who treat women badly – to stop! *And* all those women who can help it to stop to do so.

Janet, Manchester

The balancing of man and woman is not just their coming together, but also their staying separate. The process is two contradictory things happening at the same time. The difference and sameness of man and woman must be simultaneously maintained. (Ray Grigg, The Tao of Relationships*)*

Unity of all people. Love and respect for planet Earth. For people to see she is a living entity, which is in need of healing.

Yvonne, Bognor Regis

Virginia Woolf once said 'Women . . . you have never produced a Shakespeare . . . what is your excuse?' More female genius, more heroes, more forward thinking. POLITICAL ACTION. Bill of rights. More export industry encouraged. More part-time work/flexi-hours – no unemployed and lots of shared work. One-year community service obligatory. Crèche facilities. Less service industry.

F.M., London

Recognition of the work done by pro-feminist men against sexism!

M.L.

Anonymous: Prolific female author. Has written hundreds of thousands of books, articles, poems essays, memos, broadsides, and treatises. Under this name many women for centuries have written, published or produced art, either deliberately to avoid the problems and punishments awaiting the woman artist or by default because their names were lost or forgotten. (Cheris Kramarae and Paula A Treichler, A Feminist Dictionary*)*

Paternity leave in significant amounts. To make sure schoolgirls are encouraged to aim for demanding careers and science. The job of secretary not to be universally thought of as female – this degrades their work and keeps pay low. Scrapping of the national lottery which taxes the poor and stupid.

Sophie, High Wycombe

An end to animal cruelty. Respect for the environment. Tougher penalties for rapists, telephone pests, stalkers, etc.

Andrea, Hull

More information on child care for single mothers on income support, who want further education. Also for men to take women more seriously! Most (not all) men still live in the stone age. P.S. I thought the *First Sex* series made a lot of positive spirit and I'm sure there's a lot of women who feel the same way as I do!

S.M., West Midlands

There have been only twenty-four female heads of state or government, nine presidents and fifteen prime ministers, in the entire world this century. Half have been elected since 1990.

At the end of 1994 ten women were heading their governments – a number unprecedented in history.

Please can we females have one title to equal the MR of a man, whose marital status is a mystery unless asked. When the form fillers say 'Are you Mrs, Miss or Ms' it infuriates me!

Iris, Bath

I want to be safe at night so that to cycle would be a choice. I want to be taken seriously. I want all our restrictions, so clearly emphasised by the media, to be gone. I want to be safe, to be without fear of molestation on a crowded tube, in the cinema, on the street (all three have happened). I want not to have been orally raped at the age of ten in my own home. I want my daughters to be able to run free.

Lucy, London SE5

Breast screening for all women over 30. Choices of treatment for cancer. A flat stomach. To win the lottery.

Debbie, Freisham

Sometimes I wonder if men and women really suit each other. Perhaps they should live next door and just visit now and then. (Katharine Hepburn, actress)

142

More courtesy/consideration by, particularly male, drivers. Girls in senior schools shouldn't have to wear gym knickers – skirts would be preferable. My daughter is in lower school and feels very strongly.

More and easier support from courts re divorce – so much red tape is costly.

H.F., Solihull

I would like the government to show active support for breast-feeding – as a health and social issue. At the moment they seem to be married to Cow & Gate etc.

Emily, London W2

Cheaper clothes and shoes.

The Girls, Kent

The British class system has made how you look into one of the totems . . . You must be careful that how you look doesn't stop them from hearing what you say, which they barely do anyway. (Barbara Follett, founder of Emily's List UK)

I want a world with no wars. Religion's about life. Why can't people accept other religions and get on with their own? Get rid of nuclear weapons before someone makes a mistake!

Sami, Crawley

Clean air. Properly co-ordinated and cheap public transport, less cars, no more roads built. Abolition of nuclear power industry – don't privatise power stations! Global co-operation to attain peace, end the Bosnian and Chechnian wars. Men who like and understand women. Men who are more like women! Tolerance, understanding and more love.

Sam, London NW5

I want people to stop assuming that because I am 'big' (1) I eat too much,; (2) I subconsciously want to lose weight; (3) I am stupid; (4) I have no muscles, and that what I need is a man!

Sarah, Bolton

According to the Eating Disorders Association, 2 per cent of all young women in the UK suffer from anorexia or bulimia, ten times the figure for young men. Of these women, 10 per cent will die either from starvation or suicide.

More of a voice! I would like local groups to be set up where women can meet to voice their concerns/fears/needs, etc. A sort of women's 'forum'. Another place/forum where they can go to hear what's important – e.g. danger to them and children of pollutants – explain why dangerous.

Stan, London

EDUCATION – I teach about sexism as a drama teacher – why does it not come under the National Curriculum? There should be training for teachers to teach our young people about sexism and positive thinking for/towards women. I am sick of still tolerating it.

Sarah, Walden

I want the same recognition my three brothers get from my father. I also want my independence back!!

Sanjit, Telford

The subject is how to break a mold of discourse, how little by little minds change, but that they do change. (Adrienne Rich, poet)

145

San-pro on the NHS (i.e. free!) All women to remember that Norma Jean was a size 16, i.e. be proud of your body. Respect for the choice of childlessness.

P.M.B., Cambridge

I want to be taken seriously as a mature experienced woman. To have a feminine point of view given as much credence and consideration by the world, its leaders and administrators, as any other.

Edna, Isleworth

I would like assertive women to be treated with the same respect as assertive men.

Lynne, Folkestone

The proportion of women aged between 16 and 49 who said that they expected to remain childless doubled between 1986 and 1991, from 5 per cent to 10 per cent.

More trees for our future – we need to breathe, and we need forests and green places to put us in touch with the earth again.

S.N., St Andrews

To have *real* equality in our society, in fact the women to be 51 per cent in control as we run things so much better than the men! For all races, creeds and persuasions, including sexual, to accept each other. For green issues to be top of the political agenda. For the anorexic-inducing fashion industry to be seen for what it is.

Frannie, London SW6

Equal opportunities between people who have cars and people who don't. The implications of this would not fit on this card.

Nicky, Liverpool

32 per cent of women report using bottled or filtered water because they think the quality of tap water is too poor.

I just want to be at peace with myself, to take stock and begin to heal. Maybe that is what we all need.

Alana, Bath

I want to see more women playing interesting parts in films, rather than just acting the love interest for the hero. The majority of female parts are just looking pretty while the men do their stuff – and why is it that if women do actually fight they are portrayed as evil or disturbed while men who fight are given praise and adoration? We are not bimbos!

Olivia, London N4

I want a return to the kind of chivalry which has been killed by rampant feminism. Men and women are equally important but they are not the same and never will be, neither are they interchangeable.

Carole, Solihull

Women are never the right age. We're too young, we're too old. We're too thin. We're too fat. We wear too much make-up, we don't wear enough. We're too flashy in our dress, we don't take enough care. There isn't a thing we can do that's right. (Dawn Primarolo, Labour MP)

TRUTH! From the government, from corporate owners: whose interests do they have at stake? Truth about the dangers of the food dished up by supermarkets and portrayed as healthy! What about those pesticides and genetic manipulation?

Sian, London SE4

No more apologies for who we are, or the shape of our bodies, or the way we talk (words we use), and no more fear, to go or speak out. Plus a socialist government and a Labour that is Labour (not Conservative).

Stephanie, Cumbria

To be able to discover what I am, what to be a woman means, and not to have definitions imposed on me from outside.

G.F., Devon

I can't change my sex. But you can change your policy. (Helen Kirkpatrick, foreign correspondent, journalist)

Less corruption; a shift in values from sheer profit to a more considered approach; more honesty, both in public life and between people; equal opportunities.

Ruth Willis, civil servant

Men to stop considering women office workers to be domestic servants who should wait on them with cups of tea/coffee, etc. Also real pay, not lip service, and less female age discrimination in offices.

Sheila, Stretton

I want to pursue my happy life looking after my husband, three teenage children, assorted animals, garden and allotments, be able to visit my elderly mother and disabled friend, have my hobbies of music, arts and crafts, walks, be involved in environmental issues and voluntary work, manage on the money available (my husband's income), take the children to all their activities, have some time to myself without being made to feel guilty and a non-member of society because I do not do paid work.

Anon.

Black women in Britain to be more visible . . . in positions of power . . . MPs, civil service, local authorities; private industries. Positive action in breaking through the ceiling.

Jenni, Manchester

In the end, anti-black, anti-female, and all forms of discrimination are equivalent to the same thing – anti-humanism. (Shirley Chisholm, US politician, Member of Congress)

An election where all the parties' candidates must be female to redress the balance of the last 80 years' male domination. Legislation and education to create a clean environment.

Louise, London SW14

I don't want equality – I want women replacing men in all the power positions in the world and a total ban on arms and related equipment manufacture throughout the world. That is the only way we are ever going to create peace, and save the planet.

Marion, Essex

Help and encouragement to bring up our sons to channel their aggression more constructively. With changing social patterns, should men adopt their wife's surname upon marriage, so that all children retain their mother's rather than their father's name?

J.C.B., Droitwich

Men are taught to apologise for their weaknesses, women for their strengths. (Lois Wyse, advertising executive)

A general election. Properly subsidised public transport. Nursery place for every child. Environmental issues placed at top of political agenda. Paternity leave for dads. Parentcraft classes in school for all. Action on racism. More money for education.

Sue Caro, assistant editor in broadcasting

A more positive attitude towards parenting taken by fathers and employers, to make for increased equality in the home and the workplace. Mothers are not born, they evolve through necessity. So could men.

Ann, Derbyshire

I want to walk safely alone in town and country. I want my granddaughters to be able to cycle to the country unchaperoned as I did as a child.

Daphne, Norfolk

Happy, healthy children. To keep a career in spite of being a mother. For the men I work with to take me seriously. Such brilliant public transport that I'm not even tempted to use my car.

Sara, London W3

Nearly a fifth (20 per cent) of women in England and Wales feel 'very' or' fairly' unsafe when alone in their own homes at night, compared with only 4 per cent of men.

A woman and a man in equal power choosing TV programmes based on a more enlightened understanding of what a human being is and is capable of. More women programmes on the telly, i.e. more women's debates – all women or maybe one or two men. More women's opinions. More women's space. Women's pubs. More TV programmes written by women – plays, films, serials, etc. depicting things from a female perspective.

Linda, Cornwall

Freedom to be ourselves – to go where we want, wear what we want, say and do what we want, without fear of attack, abuse, being put down. Men have these freedoms. Equality in reality, not just in law. This means men caring for others and not just expecting others to care for them.

Marilyn, Birmingham

Less male attitudes in government – what about more independent MPs? Pay MPs more and expect higher qualifications and standards. Publish their CVs. No paid outside interests – they can donate time to charities if they want to keep up their skills.

Anon.

Dame Barbara Cartland published her first novel in 1922 and is now listed as the bestselling author of all time with over 600 million copies of her novels in print. She writes an average of 23 books each year.

... to shake this government + all politicians to wake them up to what they are doing to this generation and future generations. The lack of hope for the future is destroying our once great country!

Jennifer, Norwich
x

P.S.
Love + happiness for all would do nicely too!

Janis Goodman, cartoonist

No war. Pollution-free air. A clean environment. Low-cost psychotherapy. Love and happiness. Better understanding between men and women. Education. A spiritually evolved planet.

C.G., Hampshire

Yearly screening for breast and ovarian cancer for 50+ women. Job opportunities – 50+ women have lots to offer in the way of skills and experience. Government action on our polluted environment.

V.V., Reading

As a lesbian paying into a local government pension fund I would like equal rights so that in the event of my death, my partner will receive a pension. To be able to set up lesbian and gay young people's groups without the major obstacles from bigots who hold so much power.

G.B., London SE27

A major survey has revealed that almost 25 per cent of multinationals, 'are now prepared to recognise same-sex partners' when recruiting men and women for jobs in Europe. Covering nearly 200 companies active in 14 countries, Mobil Europe's data-sharing study reveals a radical shift in corporate attitudes.

Reform pornography/obliterate homelessness/no wars/tax on men/action on racism, sexism, homophobia etc./egalitarianism/free transport and more of it. Removal of the decrepit justice system and its judges. Education of men in their true responsibilities. Fairness/equal pay/equal jobs/ 50 per cent representation in government (all parties)/ true investment in the country and its people/access for people with disabilities/ excellent education for all and free/child care, 24 hours from birth (if required)/a lot less media crap aimed at women and their image/less stress and guilt/no monarchy/true socialism and equality/more for the poor and less for the rich.

Sian, London

Power to women! No more violence against women and children. An end to rape, sexual abuse, genital (and other) mutilation, unnecessary mastectomies and hysterectomies, bodily 'enhancement', male gynaecologists, etc. etc. An end to patriarchy, power to women.

Jenny, Thornhill, Dumfriesshire

(1) Respect of human rights as an individual's fundamental right; (2) Equality – non-discrimination at all times, on every level and across all groups/communities; (3) A women's approach to achieving peace.

Wendy, Twickenham, Middlesex

In 1993 there were nearly 24 million women aged 16 and over in the United Kingdom, outnumbering men by 1.5 million.

The trillions of dollars/pounds that are spent on 'offence'/'defence' budget to be used positively to help people grow their own food, live a healthy, safe life, and be good ancestors for our kids.

Jeni, Suffolk

I want men to stop trying to chat me up on the train! I want to be able to get bras in my size without having to pay a fortune!

S.C.D., London SE9

The banks to stop ripping off the Third World. Unity in diversity. The freedom to roam. Free festivals. More trees, flowers, beauty. Guns etc. to ploughshares. Freedom for the battery hen, pig, cow, calf, for the tribes from all over the world. An end to power-crazed despots and their crimes against the living. Truth, kindness, compassion. I'd like to live in a tribal situation rather than as a lone housewife, mother. End to money and on to LETS. Leaders who speak the truth.

Maggie, Shetland

The idea of strictly minding our own business is moldy rubbish. Who could be so selfish? (Myrtie Barker, columnist)

Men who know what to do to satisfy and who don't squelch me mid-conversation. To be able to bunk [room] with any band member without other people raising eyebrows. To be allowed to age with grace and dignity, same as a man.

Noel, Tennessee, USA

Maternity/paternity rights along the lines of those in Sweden. For parenting to be recognised as the most important job you can do. Improved public transport; less cars. A peaceful, caring, accepting community. Less emphasis on success, money and power/the work culture.

Judith, Edinburgh

Respect! A voice! Recognition! Position!

F.A., London NW1

A survey carried out by GQ *magazine found that 76 per cent of men questioned think that women are nagging, 70 per cent think they are erratic, 82 per cent think they are demanding and 72 per cent think they are over-emotional. 48 per cent think that 'feminism has gone too far'.*

Cheap solar energy for all, 'The Zine' to be made again. Readily available compost toilets? To be able to swim in the sea with my son safely. More time for papier mâché painting, walks on the moor. No government, or at least a totally different one. No animal testing at all. More organic vegetables and alternative medicine. Everyone to become vegans. No more animal/human/environmental cruelty. Men to stop being sexist and getting drunk. More battered wives hostels. Plymouth women's centre to reopen. Legislation of cannabis. A decent bloke. Another baby? Freedom to live how we want (peacefully). To be a traveller. Happy kind people. No more cars. No pornography.

Tabitha, Devon

To have women's issues genuinely listened to, recognised and taken into account in the political, economic and policy-making areas.

Christine, Kent

Equality in politics, work, education, the world. An end to violence against women and to war. A halt to the pollution destroying the world and the greed and domination of multinational companies. An end to the unfair trade/aid relationship between North and South.

Shirley, Edinburgh

Only seven out of the ninety-nine ministers in the Conservative government are women – the lowest proportion in any government in Europe.

Perfect health for everyone. A welfare state that ensures health and welfare for all. An end to the fear of nuclear war. For the raping and killing to stop in Eastern Europe (and everywhere). For England to vote in a Labour or a Liberal government. Rights for women in all countries especially Muslim ones. No new roads, more public transport, less cars. An end to fear of violence.

Zia, Bath

We need more safe playspace for older kids, e.g. BMX/skateboard/rollerblade park; we need an evening coffee bar *à la* Italian ones we had in '50s, '60s and '70s with jukeboxes and pin-tables for young teens.

C.W., Cumbria

Peace. Environment to be looked after. Recycling to be encouraged. No violence. No discrimination. Justice. A healthy world for children. Happy couples. Better jobs. For people to be more educated on sex, life matters and the environment. Truthful politicians.

Jane, Harrogate

Thousands upon thousands of persons have studied disease. Almost no one has studied health. (Adelle Davis, nutritionist)

To re-own my power. To maintain balance between male and female energies in the world. To attain inner peace. To create a loving, peaceful world for my children.

Patricia, East Grinstead

Good health as the world's first priority.
Julie, Gloucestershire

For women to stand up for their rights without males questioning them.

M.F., Sanderstead

I don't know how many times I've been described as having my claws out, instead of saying here's a woman being robust, which is what they would say about a man. Who would describe a man's claws as being out? (Anne Clywd, Labour MP)

I just want to be wonderful. XX

Marilyn

I am 18 years old and I want to create a life for myself. I want that life to allow me to be equal to others regardless of our race, age, gender or sexuality. I want to be able to live in the world, not 'Europe' or 'the Northern Hemisphere'. I want to be part of a world community that treats everyone with care and respect, where nations embrace nations out of a willingness to help and not because of profit, duty or international security.

Ruth, Kent

Worldwide green government. Elimination of aggression, intolerance, prejudice and religion and other sources of universal instability.

Irene, Glasgow

We have all known the long loneliness and we have learned that the only solution is love and that love comes from community. (Dorothy Day, humanitarian)

Reverence for all life. Equal opportunities. No war. Co-operation and global peace. Global justice and equity, fair trade. A clean environment. No more 'roads to ruin'. Compassion in world farming. Accountability of multinationals, the World Bank, the IMF.

Hilda, Wivenhoe

A world with far fewer humans, consuming far less, destroying other species and habitats less. A society in which kids can walk to school. All of which may mean more restraints on our activities and some of our 'freedoms'.

Mrs V., Loughborough

To be able to live according to and within my feminine integrity! In other words: a world which places equal value on both masculine and feminine values i.e. co-operation and competition – more of the first! A fair and just society.

C.L.

One of the many sad results of the Industrial Revolution was that we came to depend more than ever on the intellect, and to ignore the intuition with its symbolic thinking. (Madeleine L'Engle, author)

Legislation, similar to that in Canada, where soft porn material is sold, i.e. the image covered and brand name only displayed. Less practical: ALL CAR EXHAUSTS adult month night – not buggy: quicker legislation to clean the air. Bus stops off the road kerb (see Netherlands).

B.E., London W12

A return to a place where the feminine was revered and the universal worship of the goddess.

Claire, Northern Ireland

Childbirth with no pain. Better methods of contraception. Tolerance and acceptance. People to care. Emphasis on the spiritual and emotional rather than the material. More women in influential positions.

Sharon, Brighton

In Brazil, some fathers bleed themselves during their partner's labour, to share the pain of childbirth.

The British to leave Ireland.

Carmen, London W11

I want a man to look after, so I can cook and clean for him and just be there for him. In return he should be kind and gentle and show me some respect.

Silvia, London E11

Looking around at all the options I think I want it all. Knowing that this is impossible I basically want to be contented and to always be learning something new.

Sharon, Potters Par

In 1993 UK women spent an average of 8.44 hours per week cleaning the house. UK men spent an average of 3.56 hours.

Society's attitudes to change so that my thirteen-year-old daughter can be proud of her lesbian mother rather than being scared to death that her friends will find out.

Susan, Manchester

The certainty that women never again need beg for a hearing, nor for credence to be given. That women must now make a great noise, filling the universe with its sound, which will not die until the world is dry, and all are perished – Babycham is not enough.

Benedicta, Richmond, Surrey

I want to ban the pictorial prostitution of women in advertising, selling anything from newspapers to hub caps. It demeans all of us.

Patricia, Nottingham

The World Bank estimates that in the industrialised countries, rape and domestic violence account for almost one in every five healthy years of life lost to women aged fifteen to forty-four.

Less to do!

Monica, London SE20

Equal pay for work of equal value and an explosion of this still prevalent myth that men should earn more than women. I am currently suing for equal pay at an industrial tribunal!

Nicola, Shropshire

Acknowledgement that being a woman means you can hold your own, be strong, be weak, be gorgeous, be a bitch, be sexual but not want sex, be respected to the highest and be treated with a higher regard than a second-class citizen.

Imogen, Somerset

In the UK women's pay is, on average, only 80 per cent of men's.

Acceptance and respect for 'fat' people. Clothes more widely available for bigger people – we don't want to wear tents; just because we are big doesn't mean we aren't beautiful.

Rachel, Coventry

Lessons of love: schools offer a very limited sex education programme. I believe that discussions on love and relationships and educating children to express themselves emotionally are incredibly important to the well-being of the future culture.

Lisa, Hertfordshire

I'm 15. I want the government to be not corrupt. I want peace among all nations. Animals should be decently treated – that means no more messing with their various food chains. We should look after our world. I want to love and be loved. Plus adequate student grants.

Martha, Norwich

Just three minutes of gazing at pictures of skinny, smooth-skinned models in women's magazines causes seven out of ten women to experience feelings of depression, stress, guilt and shame.

Paternity leave, strong single women role models, affordable housing, communications at work, allowing of feelings, mediation not litigation, no war, personal development for all, understanding, listening.

Maggie Sawkins, artist

More options on child care for working mothers.
D.L.C., London NW7

I want to be able to refuse a drink when offered (by a man) without being pushed around for the rest of the evening; to enjoy the same social status as men and do what they do without being punished for it by name calling and the ever-present threat of sexual violence; to be able to dance without being grabbed like the star attraction at a meat market; non-feminist women to stop trying to harm the movement.
Claire, Rotherham

To not feel obliged to take a man's name on marrying him. To not feel expected to have children. To feel safe to walk the streets by night.
Charlotte, Oxfordshire

I have sometimes compared it [women's liberation] in its slowness to the movements of a glacier but like a glacier it was ceaseless and irresistible. (Millicent Fawcett, leading women's suffrage campaigner in early 1900s)

I want to see education at all levels, including adult education, properly funded in this country and student grants made available to all who need them, at a level where it is possible to live on them. I want to see a new UK government a.s.a.p. and a start made on righting the wrongs this current bunch of idiots have been up to.

I would also like to meet an intelligent, attractive, interesting lover before I'm 30 (six months to go).

I.D., Canterbury

An end to violence against all women, all living creatures and the earth. Peace of mind, body and soul. An end to poverty. Quality of living for all. Universal love. Laughter. A trip in a flying saucer. Creativity.

I.S., Glasgow

My opinions to count towards government's decision making. To take politics out of government.

Karen, Northamptonshire

In a world ranking of women's access to political power, UNICEF's Progress of Nations *report (June 1995) finds that worldwide only one elected politician in nine is a woman.*

Political asylum for women fleeing 'cultural violence' (e.g. female genital mutilation, violent enforcement of dress codes: Hijab).
A clear and definitive UN policy/EU policy on women's human rights here and abroad.
UK: a change to immigration rules (at present women are forced to stay in violent marriages or face deportation).
Quotas in politics and the professions (to ensure equal numbers of men and women).

A.H., Bradford

A world where there is the same amount of respect paid to each woman as there is for men.

J.T-P., Shropshire

I don't want to be responsible for paying all this mortgage and bringing up a child – 'cos I work and he doesn't. I'm not Superwoman!
I want equal rights.
I want good health care.
I want someone to listen.

P.D.P., Leeds

Official figures for refugees suggest there are at least 17 million globally – people displaced from their own country as a result of war, famine and political persecution. 80 per cent of refugees are women and children.

More teaching in schools about personal relationships, spiritual (non-sectarian) values and counselling, as many parents are not educated enough themselves in these areas to help their children adequately. Also, more counselling, patient consultation in mental institutions, by awake and aware people.

Moira, Huddersfield

At the moment I'm studying for my HNC in graphic design. I am a young mum in a good steady relationship and I feel as though I'm being kicked in the teeth. I can't go full time – lack of childminding fees, etc. – and on a part-time course I get no grant and my partner is on a low wage. I can't get sponsored as I would have to work summer holidays. Catch 22. I only want to retain my mental independence.

J.E.N, Oxfordshire

I want world leaders and multinationals to start taking global environmental problems seriously, and also to stop blaming the South for problems caused by the North.

Jill, London SE11

Despite some progress made in specific areas since 1989, one-third of lone parents still give lack of child care as the main reason for not working, and the majority of these cite cost as the prime obstacle.

Respect for the earth, water, air and all living things. Status as part of humanity no unimportant 'Other'. Energy put into education, health and love, not war, alienation and fear.

Moira Henderson, carpentry student

Recognition of the unique qualities women can and do bring to society and industry. An end to barriers created by gender stereotyping and narrow-minded men.

Lucky, Ampthill

Recognition that the virgin forests of the world are being destroyed by the increase in paper consumption. More recycling and non-wood paper. Less use of obscene disposable paper products made from forests.

Pat, London NW6

I would love a national campaign to encourage kids to insist that they be walked to school, for health and environmental reasons. Also, to stop people sitting in their cars with engines running either to keep warm, or now with air conditioning available to keep cool.

Sue, Romford

In 1995, each person in the UK used approximately 200 kilograms of paper. The average African woman uses 13 kilograms of paper in a year.

Kate Taylor, illustrator

Respect for celibacy.

J.A.P., London N1

Women to cease deriving satisfaction from the sorrows/downfalls of other women. Mothers to raise their sons to respect women and regard both sexes as equal and a compatible partnership.

If these two points could be voiced more loudly in talk shows/written articles, etc. maybe women would realise they are their own worst enemy.

Jean, Austria

For men and women to realise they are different to each other and to enjoy those differences and not rebel against them. Time – to enjoy.

June, Hove

94 per cent of women describe very close, important, and enjoyable friendships with other women.

A room (flat, preferably) of my own. The twentieth century equivalent of £100 a year and my own weekly column in the Sunday supplements. More generally, a stronger feminist consciousness amongst women and for men young and old to stop telling me feminism goes too far.

Ruth, London N2

To be eligible for fertility treatment on the NHS even though I'm 42. I've only been married for two years and haven't had any success so far. We keep practising, though!

Anon.

Not equality because if you want it, you don't feel equal in the first place. Peace, gentleness, families to be together, encouragement for women to be inspirational not a temptation.

Jan, London SW7

Focus on the needs of the single, widowed, divorced woman, often a 'carer', often in poverty, often lonely – provision of shared housing; no extra prices for single rooms in hotels, for holidays. Crèches. Respect.

M.S., Harrogate

In 1992, seven US women aged between 50 and 59 became pregnant after successful operations grafted the fertilised eggs of a younger donor.

For the nuclear industry to be closed down. Certainly *not* for it to be privatised. For us to stop poisoning the planet. A green and socialist (not necessarily Labour) government. Better films and TV programmes, more featuring strong older women. Longer holidays. Supermodels woman-size.

Alice, London SE5

I want to be able to telephone Yugoslavia from Croatia (and vice versa). Because of the war, telephone contact is denied. I want all peace negotiating teams in former Yugoslavia to include women. I want the arms industry to stop. I want lesbians to have equal rights.

Rachel, Zagreb

I want to do my doctorate. I want to further my education but there is no money to finance it. I want to see more women in further education but this will never happen if the financial crisis continues and women remain under-educated . . . I want to study, I want to learn, I want to know . . .

Irene, Stirlingshire

The number of students enrolled on further education courses in the UK rose by 333,000 between 1980/81 and 1988/89. Female students accounted for over 80 per cent of this increase.

I want to stop the systematic ghettoisation of the urban housing estates on the fringes of our major cities. Young people from these areas should be given a voice in local and central government. There, apathy breeds discontent and violence. It destroys lives and casts a blight on the human spirit. Such places should shame politicians into action, as to ignore them is to ignore our future.

Jean, Liverpool

Improved educational provision for women of all ages, classes and colour etc. I want to be part of world conferences on women. I want to be respected and admired instead of 'put down' by others. I want to be free of the limitations I create in my own mind.

Jo, Huddersfield

An improvement in opportunities for women returning to work. At present women who chose during the '70s/early '80s to stay at home with children or who were trapped by convention or by poorer maternity laws to 'put their husbands' job first' are now trapped by the ageism which will not accept them re-entering the job market in their forties. Until this issue is addressed women will not even get fair opportunities.

K.D.N., Maidenhead

The economist Heather Joshi has estimated that a mother loses up to 57 per cent of her potential lifetime earnings compared to a woman who has no children.

I long for compassion to be the hallmark of our society – I long to see men honouring women and women honouring men – I long to see gentleness, tenderness and integrity in relationships between sexes, and between races and people of all ages.

Pippa, Liverpool

I want the average pay for women workers to be the same as the average pay for male workers. I want the trade unions to deal with harassment with firmness and speed.

K.F. Glasgow

£4.15 per hour minimum wage. Trade Union rights restored from day one. Good Trade Union education courses and updates on employment legislation, sick pay benefits and to pay National Insurance contributions.

P.B. Shotton, Clwyd

In 1993 the UK government abolished the Wages Councils which gave minimum wage level protection to millions of workers – three-quarters of whom were women.

In journalism, I see over-confident young men given opportunities denied to more competent, less pushy women. I want women to gain the confidence to match their abilities. As for me, I'd like radio editors to stop saying how good my reporting would be if only I'd deepen my voice just a little.

Lindsey, London N16

Silence. Space. Self-possession. A society that can no longer take shopping seriously.

Gillian, Durham

Cheap, equitable, excellent neighbourhood day care for our children so we can combine our home and public lives freely and without guilt.

Lucy, London WC2

70 per cent of health care for elderly people is provided by women at home. 65 per cent of under-5s whose parents work are cared for by relatives, neighbours or friends.

To be able to walk or drive in London without having to wear a mask because the air is not fit to breathe. For men to understand that the first Goddesses were women – it hasn't always been a man's world.

Fiona May, temp. secretary/PA

Honesty; trust.

Janet, Upminster

Clean air! Zero violence against women. Free public transport. No unrecyclable packaging. Dry toilets in every home. End of war anywhere. Cheap organic food.

Stefania, London SE5

I want the secretary of the Nolan Committee (and others of his ilk) to know (without having to be told) that it is contemptuous to reply to a woman who has taken the trouble to write to him, signing the communication 'yours faithfully, S. Davison (Miss)' with a letter addressed to 'S. Davison. Esq.' and commencing 'Dear Sir'!

Suzanne, London E17

At least eight in ten women think that something should be done about issues such as toxic and radioactive waste, chemical pollution of seas and rivers, and sewage on beaches.

I want to be abducted by aliens and travel to a new world. I would like communism to end in China and more consideration, money and help to be given to orphanages in China.

Rita, Epsom

More cubicles in women's public toilets to eliminate the queues. Stop all junk mail! More space to write my address!

A.C., Solihull

Funding for education
Freedom of information
Proportional representation
Women in power
Punishment to fit the crime
Better maternity schemes
Peace, love and happiness

Andrea, London N1

On average, women spend twice as long in toilet cubicles than men, yet Health and Safety regulations require only equal numbers of cubicles.

For me: to 'retire' from work – or just work half of the year but with a secure future/income. Travel/revisit places. Write, research (PhD). Pursue my own interests. Run a motel, maybe. For me and the world: less pollution, less pain, less poverty and violence, end to animal suffering.

L.G., South Glamorgan

Child-centred education – teach about different cultures, nature, self-worth and value.
Breast-feeding at board meetings.
Strong feminine role models (not the Maggie T. type)
Peace and love between women and men and all people.
Songs about being joyous and happy in myself/ourselves with no reference to (romantic) love.
Herstory not history.
Respect for children.

Miranda, London W14

Respect for *all* life. Immediate cessation of polluting activities. Worldwide nuclear disarming and decommissioning of nuclear power stations.

C.T., London N1

NASA, Ariane and Soyuz rockets, shuttles and boosters produce more chlorine-containing compounds that destroy the ozone layer than all the aerosol production in the world.

Protect insect diversity (I am an ecologist and an entomologist).
Adequate recycling.
The right to education for all.
Unpolluted air to breathe.
Pesticide-residue-free food to eat.
Ecological science taught at primary level and right through school as a compulsory subject, not necessarily assessed.
World co-operation on all issues.
Crèches for all mothers.

Sharon, Lancaster

Public relations – so that the numerous voices of the environmental lobby have a say in governmental policy making.

Pam, Penzance

An interesting, challenging job at a competitive rate of pay without having to fight extra hard because I am female. More recycling facilities, especially for plastics. Less pressure to get married and have children.

Jane, London

Whatever women do they must do twice as well as men to be thought half as good. Luckily this is not difficult. (Charlotte Whitton, writer)

An end to private education. One education system for all children, regardless of income of parents. Plus, a higher ratio of teachers to pupils in class (e.g. one teacher to 15 pupils). I am a parent of a 14-year-old.

Ella, London

I want the fear taken out of the perceptions of mental illness.
Contentment, no war, no racism.
I want everyone to realise that we are joined together and joined to the planet.
Equal opportunities for all, including disabled.
I want the man I love to love me back.
I want therapy to be available, free, to all who need it.

Amanda, Aviemore

Financial help for older people who become disabled after the age of 25 years to retrain and/or for starting businesses of their own. Mandatory grants for disabled people to attend college part-time. A legal right for disabled people to attend all institutions of higher education.

J.T., Truro

Four and a half million disabled adults live in households where there are no earners. Over 70 per cent of disabled adults were on an income 75 per cent or less than the average income.

Free sanitary protection! We don't choose to menstruate. We do choose to have sex yet can get free condoms. Space. More time alone. Childcare facilities. Free Lube. Understanding. The right to choose.

Jackie, Folkestone

More time. Another breadwinner
Hilary, Machynlleth, Powys

To be included as equal partner – especially to use inclusive language and images.

Annette, London

I want the freedom to recognise and rejoice in the desires of my own heart, and the courage to follow my star. And I want it for *you* too! So that together we may fly with the Angels and touch the sun!

Mo, Stafford

60 per cent of people in the world believe in angels.

1. Prevention of cancers related to women by: Mammograms, cervical smears, ultrasound scans – yearly and for women aged over 20.
2. Stop the production of rayon and using it in tampons in UK, as they have in USA, Canada and Australia.
3. I want women at work to stop making me feel guilty because my children are ill.

R.M., Bradford

I want us to live with the natural world, not against it. An end to embryo research and genetic engineering. To be safe to walk outside – day or night – and safe to leave windows open. I want world peace and refugees to be allowed to be helped. Freedom to adopt unwanted/war children across borders. Freedom to be a mother and/or a career woman, i.e. one salary can support a home so women are not forced away from home to work. I want to be able to buy and eat and drink food and water free from chemical additives. I want worldwide *local* government. I want tyrants all put together in a cage with weapons – a damage limitation exercise. Anyone may have a temporary visit. I want this world to learn positive sexual practices. I want alcohol and tobacco made very difficult to obtain and socially unacceptable.

Kate, London W1

Health is not simply the absence of sickness. (Hannah Green, writer)

No tax on sanitary products. More family allowance so we can stay at home with our children instead of working and trying to sort out child care. Fewer working hours in a week so we don't spend more time there than with our husbands/partners. A four-day work/three-day off week.

Marnie, Cardiff

I want media representation of women as strong individuals with a need to take care of their physical, mental and spiritual health, not figure-obsessed victims of male advertising.

K.W., London SW8

World peace, and an end to poverty and homelessness.

Clare, Newcastle

Alice Mahon MP comments that every time she asks a question, 'it's written up as an outburst. Men ask questions and I make outbursts.'

Financial independence and Tantric sex. I want to be paid for the work that I do. I want equal rights. I want a feminine response to environmental issues. I want to have *fun*.

Tessa, London, NW1

As a woman of the '90s I want to be respected and recognised for my own talents and skills, not as my father's daughter or my husband's wife. I also want more opportunity and choice for women in their career, education and home life.

Yasmin, Liverpool

A vegan world – less exploitation and hunger. Men's bodies and hearts but not their egotism. Capitalism to be overthrown and everything to be shared equally. To be a good architect.
Pamela, Lancaster

Between 1960 and 1990, the number of working women rose by 34 per cent, while the number of working men fell by 20 per cent.

I want the needs of black and Asian women to be taken seriously. Legislation against the interests of women in our community needs to be opposed by all women.

Yasmin, London W3

Not to feel threatened when walking around. To be given allowances for suffering from monthly periods.

Anon.

I want the discrimination black women work hard to overcome acknowledged. I want their/our/my achievements and contribution to the British society recognised through better jobs, better child care and some thanks.

Alexis, Bexleyheath

The 1993 Annual Guide to the Best of British Women, *listing nearly 1,400 of the most successful women in the country in over 175 categories, lists details of only 18 successful black women, and nine of those worked in the music industry.*

More public transport. A proper NHS and education system. Basically, an end to all this market forces nonsense!!

A.C., Birmingham

Greater safety on the streets – greater deterrents for crime of a sexual nature. Greater fairness in the legal system – overhaul of male-orientated guidelines. Luxury tax removed from sanitary protection.

Nicky, Strathbungo

More funding for women artists of all disciplines to train internationally.

Lynne, Newcastle

Evelyn Glennie OBE is the world's first full-time solo percussionist. A regular performer with all Britain's major symphony and chamber orchestras, in 1989 she gave the first ever solo percussion recital in the history of the Promende concerts. She is profoundly deaf.

Clean air – which will only come with admission that something has to be done about transportation. Proper education – no fear of learning. For women to have the courage to be recognised as women, not women trying to be men in a foolish patriarchal society, for only then will harmony be restored. The hope for any kind of future for my children.

Dorian, Wiltshire

Equality, fair pay and for men to have babies and periods.

Marian, Sutton Coldfield

A return of the ancient female wisdom, i.e. spiritual values instead of material values. Peace worldwide. Women in all positions where men have control. A clean and healthy environment. Freedom from hunger. Rights for animals – no factory farming. Complementary medicine to be available on the NHS. Steiner education available to all children.

Gill, Bristol

The present evolution of women . . . is to my mind the most profound revolution that highly developed societies will have to contend with. (Françoise Giraud, Swiss politician and Minister of Women)

I want to stop the systematic ghettoisation of the urban housing estates on the fringes of our major cities. Young people from these areas should be given a voice in local and central government. There, apathy breeds discontent and violence. It destroys lives and casts a blight on the human spirit. Such places should shame politicians into action, as to ignore them is to ignore our future.

Jean, Liverpool

Strange as it may seem I want the same as men, it's just that men are never expected to have to make the choices that women are.

Julie, Gwynedd

We need to restore balance to the universe – between the feminine and masculine; the spiritual and material. We need to move away from ignorance to knowledge; from darkness to light and from bondage to freedom. This can only come into being when we recognise the awesome potential within ourselves as women. The essence of femaleness needs to be celebrated; the power and love of the goddess lies within each of us. If we can grow stronger through this consciousness then we can move towards healing, reconnecting and becoming whole.

Rehana, London N15

If de furst woman God ever made was strong enough to turn the world upside down all alone, dese women togedder ought to be able to turn it back, and get it right side up again. (Sojourner Truth, abolitionist)

Men and the employers of men to realise their responsibilities as parents from birth onwards and act positively to improve the fathering role. Elle McPherson's legs!

J.P., Hertford

I want to be liked by men. I want them to see us as their friends not their enemies (threatening to them). I want the men to listen and be interested and therefore make me feel special, human. I want women to be listened to, acknowledged.

Penny, Liverpool

A man who actually likes women. A sensitive, caring, unselfish man who sees his chosen partner as a friend and takes the entering into of a relationship seriously and family unity, love and respect as the most important foundations of a successful partnership and the sound building blocks for a stable society.

S.W., Weymouth

81 per cent of women questioned say they would like men to listen with more interest in what they are saying, to take their thoughts more seriously, and give more intelligent feedback.

I desperately want a clean environment for my children and theirs. And this includes the right to unadulterated foods: organic vegetables, uninjected meat and dairy produce without added hormones.

K.Z., Buckinghamshire

Equal opportunities. Recognition of the work of motherhood. Twenty-four-hour nurseries. Chemical castration for repeating rapists. Life sentences meaning Life. Life for carrying offensive weapons. Peace.

E.R.N., London SW13

A change in culture in governing organisations. Turn materialism and destruction to co-operation and care for the quality of life. A sense of safety at home and on the streets and transport. Less stress, shorter working hours. More trees and green spaces. Greater understanding between men and women.

Maddy, London SW2

The Tao is called the Great Mother: empty yet inexhaustible, it gives birth to infinite worlds. It is always present within you. You can use it anyway you want. (Tao Te Ching)

1. More women in positions of power.
2. Changes in male culture.
3. A more women-centred society.
4. Better health care, education and public transport.
5. No pollution.
6. Smaller and cheaper portions in restaurants.
7. M&S underwear which stays in stock for more than a year.

Lucy, London NW5

I would like to bring my children up in a society that does not revolve increasingly around *sex*. I am sick of newspapers, magazines, radio, TV and advertising sold using sex. It's boring, unhealthy and very unimaginative. Bring back censorship!

Ruth, Dundee

Worldwide recognition of the equal value and significance of women and men.
Full human rights for all women.

Barbara, Hampshire

'Sex' as we define it is part of the whole cultural picture; a woman's place in sex mirrors her place in the rest of society. (Shere Hite, women's researcher and writer)

Art history to be removed from the patriarchal. There were great women artists, for example Eva Gonzales and Berthe Morisot.

Kate, Manchester

I want a good professional training to become an excellent surgeon. I want to work in a health service that provides adequate resources for everybody regardless of sex, race or age. I want to abolish gender so that everybody can live in mutual respect.

Beatrix, Rosehill

Cycle paths, especially in cities. Free nursery education, nationwide. Free high-quality parenting skills courses. More informed choice on pregnancy, childbirth and childhood vaccination. Tough legal action on abuse of women and children, particularly in pornographic videos.

Chrissy, London SE22

The Tate Gallery owns 15,000 works of art; 1,200 are by women, and on average only 30 are on display.

Most of all I would like women to feel safe and confident when they go about their daily lives – to be able to travel on buses and trains, drive alone in cars or walk along the road without fear of mugging, molestation or harassment.

Ann, Glasgow G1

I want to see characteristically female ways of working: co-operatively, creatively, flexibly, becoming the norm in professional organisations.

Wendy, Stratford-upon-Avon

I want to talk to a sympathetic mathematician because I think I can demonstrate a link between prime numbers and the coilings of the D.N.A.

Patrician, London SW6

When we take away the right to an individual name, we symbolically take away the right to be an individual. Immigration officials did this to refugees, husbands do it routinely to wives. (Erica Jong, poet and novelist)

Less scaremongering by the Media! Less pornography in video and print. Less traffic on the roads. Improved public transport systems. More focus on world needs – less on personal gain. Less alcohol, less gambling. More positives – less negatives.

Jean, Whitwick

After-school child care. Holiday playschemes. Tax relief on child care. Discouragement of 'macho' work environment and long hours accepted as the norm.

Linda, Prestatyn

To give young children a 'taste' of sign language – a 'day' in a wheelchair, etc. to make them more 'aware of all links of people and take away ignorance and fears – choice in my own health care, e.g. alternative medicine and therapies. More information on these. Proper encouragement and financial support for all to go back into education to provide better job opportunities. To feel safe walking alone anywhere (particularly in countryside for pleasure) and all of the above. Peace, education and fulfilment.

Christine, Manchester

Imagination is the highest kite one can fly. (Lauren Bacall, actress)

WHAT DO YOU WANT?

to be allowed the

space to blossom

Name ....

Address ....

Tel ....

Would you like to know more? Yes/No

WHAT WOMEN WANT

3-4 Albion Place

Galena Road

London W6 OLT

References

p.2. F.A. Premier League Survey 1995. Quoted in *Cosmopolitan*, September 1995, p.18.

p.11. 'Families' Jo Boyden with UNESCO, 1993, p.150.

p.12. Women's Environmental Network. Quoted in *Everywoman,* June 1995, p.4.

p.15. Women's National Commission report 'Women in the 90's', p.62.

p.16. Equal Opportunities Commission briefing paper, 'The Pensions Bill Implications for Sex Equality', p.1.

p.17. The British Household Panel Survey, quoted in 'Social Focus on Women' report by the Central Statistical Office, August 1995, p.51.

p.18. *Towards Equality*, The Fawcett Society newsletter, Spring 1995, p.1.

p.21. 'Gender, Poverty and Sustainable Development – Towards a holistic framework of understanding and action' Vivienne Wee and Noeleen Heyzer p.36 & p.l40. Published by Engender – Centre for Environment, Gender and Development Pte Ltd. Singapore, with funding assistance from the UNDP.

p.22. Second Report of the UK Ministerial Group on Women's Issues May 1991, p.66.

p.27. Equal Opportunities Commission Briefing paper on Education and Training p.2. Department of Education, Scottish Examination Board, Welsh Joint Education Committee & Universities Statistical Record, 1995.

p.28. Office of Population Censuses and Surveys, quoted in 'Social Focus on Women' report by the Central Statistical Office, August 1995, p.40 & p.44.

p.29. 'What in the World has the UN got to do with Women?' Labour Party report for the United Nations Fourth World Conference on Women Beijing 1995, June 1995, introduction by Clare Short, p.iii.

p.30. UNICEF pamphlet 'Education for Girls: Lifeline to Development'.

p.31. Survey by the Department of Environment,

quoted in 'Social Focus on Women' report by the Central Statistical Office August 1995, p.53.

p.35. Second report of the UK Ministerial Group on Women's Issues, May 1991, p.133.

p.36. Social Trends 1994 quoted in 'What in the World has the UN got to do with Women?' Labour Party report for the United Nations Fourth World Conference on Women Beijing 1995, June 1995, p.15.

p.37. 'What in the World has the UN got to do with Women?' Labour Party report for the United Nations Fourth World Conference on Women Beijing 1995, June 1995, introduction by Clare Short, p.iv.

p.38. UN report 'The World's Women 1995 – Trends and Statistics', p.106.

p.39. 'What in the World has the UN got to do with Women?' Labour Party report for the United Nations Fourth World Conference on Women Beijing 1995, June 1995, introduction by Clare Short , p.iv.

p.41. Equal Opportunities Commission Briefing Paper, 'National Agenda for Action – Combining Work and Family', p.4.

p.43. Forthcoming UN report, 'International Parliamentary Union and the World's Women: Trends and Statistics (1970–1995)' quoted in UN Publication 'The Advancement of Women – Notes for Speakers', p.75.

p.44. Article by Jodi Jacobsen in *People and the Planet* Vol. 5 No. 3, p.7.

p.45. *Everywoman*, November 1995, p.19.

p.46. British Crime Survey, England and Wales 1994, quoted in 'Social Focus on Women', report by the Central Statistical Office, August 1995, p.51.

p.48. *Marie-Claire*, 1995.

p.50. 'Gender, Poverty and Sustainable Development – Towards a holistic framework of understanding and action' Vivienne Wee and Noeleen Heyzer p.36. Published by Engender – Centre for Environment, Gender and Development Pte Ltd. Singapore, with funding assistance from the UNDP.

p.51. Equal Opportunities Commission Briefing Paper, 'National Agenda for Action – Combining Work and Family', p.6.

p.53. Second Report of the UK Ministerial Group on Women's Issues May 1991, p.11.

p.54. 'What in the World has the UN got to do with Women?' Labour Party report for the United Nations Fourth World Conference on Women Beijing 1995, June l995 p.l7.

p.55. Women's National Commission Report 'Women in the 90's', p.7.

p.56. 'Families' Jo Boyden with UNESCO 1993, p. 104

p.57. Department of Employment, quoted in 'Social Focus on Women' report published by the Central Statistical Office, August 1995, p.21.

p.60. 'What in the World has the UN got to do with Women?' Labour Party report for the United Nations Fourth World Conference on Women Beijing 1995, June 1995, p.17.

p.66. USA Today, quoted in *The Harper's Index Book*, p.65.

p.67. Women's National Commission, quoted in 'Report of the United Kingdom of Great Britain and Northern Ireland for the United Nations Fourth World Conference on Women, Beijing 1995', p.115.

p.70. UN Publication 'The Advancement of Women – Notes for Speakers' p.44; IFAD 'Banking on Women: Facts and Figures' press release for the publication of 'The State 0f World Rural Poverty', quoted in Un Publication 'The Advancement of Women – Notes for Speakers', p.19.

p.71. 'Families' Jo Boyden with UNESCO 1993, p.124.

p.72. 'What in the World has the UN got to do with Women?' Labour Party report for the United Nations Fourth World Conference on Women Beijing 1995, June 1995, introduction by Clare Short, p.iv.

p.74. Second Report of the UK Ministerial Group on Women's Issues, May 1991, table 11.4., p.104.

p.77. The Howard League for Penal Reform and the National Association of Probation Officers, quoted in *Cosmopolitan* magazine, July 1995, p.24.

p.78. *Everywoman*, November 1995, p.8.

p.82. 'Report to European Community Foreign Ministers of the Investigative Mission into the Treatment of Muslim Women in the Former Yugoslavia', quoted in the United Nations report, 'The World's Women 1995 – Trends and Statistics', p.164.

p.85. *Cosmopolitan*, January 1995, p.51.

p.86. Market Opinion and Research Institute (MORI) survey 'Women in the '90s' June 1995.

p.88. Shelter homeless action group, telephone correspondence, 1995.

p.89. Women's Aid Federation, telephone correspondence, 1995.

p.92. 1993 Survey by the Department of the Environment, quoted in 'Social Focus on Women', report by the Central Statistical Office, August 1995, p.53.

p.93. Equal Opportunities Commission, quoted in National Alliance of Women's Organisations, Annual Report 1993, p.1.

p.94. Market Opinion and Research Institute (MORI) survey, April/May 1991.

p.96. Shelter homeless action group, telephone correspondence, 1995.

p.97. UNICEF report, 'Progress of Nations', quoted in *People and the Planet* Vol. 4 no. 3 1995, p.3.

p.98. Equal Opportunities Commission Briefing Paper on Education and Training, p.2.

p.102. Tony Eardley, 1989, quoted by Shelter homeless action group.

p.103. Shelter homeless action group, telephone correspondence, 1995.

p.104. Survey of Disability in Great Britain 1988, Office of Population Censuses and Surveys.

p.105. Survival International.

p.106. Ganmills Ltd, personal correspondence 1995.

p.110. 'What in the World has the UN got to do with Women?' Labour Party report for the United Nations Fourth World Conference on Women Beijing 1995, June 1995, p.11.

p.111. 'What in the World has the UN got to do with Women?' Labour Party report for the United Nations Fourth World Conference on Women Beijing 1995, June 1995, p.20.

p.112. Advertisement for 'Classic Combination' clothes catalogue.

p.115. British Social Attitudes Survey 1992/93, Social and Community Planning Research.

p.119. 'Families' Jo Boyden with UNESCO 1993, p.158.

p.120. Broadcasting Standards Council study, 'Perspectives of Women in Television' 1994, quoted in 'Report of the United Kingdom of Great

Britain and Northern Ireland for the United Nations Fourth World Conference on Women, Beijing 1995', p.109

p.121. *Who's Who of Women in the Twentieth Century*, Bison Books Ltd, London 1995.

p.122. Shere Hite 'Women and Love' Survey, 1988.

p.123. Survey by the Museum of Women's Art, from information provided by the galleries.

p.126. 'What in the World has the UN got to do with Women?' Labour Party report for the United Nations Fourth World Conference on Women Beijing 1995, June 1995, introduction by Clare Short, p.iv.

p.130. 'Families' Jo Boyden with UNESCO 1993, p.143.

p.131. European Commission Network on Childcare annual report, 'Employment, Equality and Caring for Children' 1992, p.11.

p.132. 1993 study by UNESCO and Margaret Gallagher, consultant to Statistical Division of UN Secretariat, quoted in United Nations report 'The World's Women 1995 – Trends and Statistics', pp.156–7.

p.133. British Crime Survey England and Wales 1994, quoted in 'Special Focus on Women' report by the Central Statistical Office, August 1995, p.51.

p.135. 'What in the World has the UN got to do with Women?' Labour Party report for the United Nations Fourth World Conference on Women Beijing 1995, June 1995, p.18.

p.138. 'What in the World has the UN got to do with Women?' Labour Party report for the United Nations Fourth World Conference on Women Beijing 1995, June 1995 p.8. Source: Equal Opportunities Commission report, 'Labour Market Structures and Prospects for Women' 1994.

p.141. Division for the Advancement for Women of the United Nations Secretariat, quoted in United Nations report, 'The World's Women 1995 – Trends and Statistics' pp.151–2

p.146. 'Social Focus on Women' report by the Central Statistical Office, August 1995, p.16.

p.147. Department of the Environment survey 1993, quoted in 'Social Focus on Women' report by Central Statistical Office, August 1995, p.53.

p.155. British Crime Survey England and Wales 1994, quoted in 'Social Focus on Women' report by the Central Statistical Office, August 1995, p.51.

p.156. *Who's Who of Women in the Twentieth Century*, Bison Books Ltd, London 1995.

p.158. Nicola Cole, Gemini News Service, quoted in *New Internationalist*, October 1995, p.5.

p.159. 'Social Focus on Women' report by the Central Statistical Office, August 1995, p.9.

p.161. *Everywoman*, February 1995, p.4.

p.162. 'What in the World has the UN got to do with Women?' Labour Party report for the United Nations Fourth World Conference on Women Beijing 1995, June 1995, p.22.

p.167. *Mamatoto*, Virago, London 1994.

p.168. Henley Centre/Research International 1993/94, quoted by James Murphy at Marketing to Women Conference 19th October 1993.

p.169. A.M. Davies, 'Older Populations Ageing Individuals and Health for All', World Health Forum Vol. 10 1989, quoted in United Nations Publication 'The Advancement of Women – Notes for Speakers', p.40.

p.170. United Nations report, 'The World's Women 1995 – Trends and Statistics', p.127.

p.171. *Everywoman*, March 1995, p.7.

p.175. UNICEF report, 'Progress of Nations' June 1995.

p.176. 'Families' Jo Boyden with UNESCO 1993, p.126.

p.177. Women's National Commission report, 'Women in the '90s', p.17.

p.180. Women's Environmental Network paper briefing, 1993.

p.182. Shere Hite 'Women and Love' Survey, 1988.

p.183. 'Families' Jo Boyden with UNESCO 1993, p.138.

p.184. Second Report of the UK Ministerial Group on Women's Issues May 1991, p.63.

p.185. Equal Opportunities Commission Briefing Paper, 'National Agenda for Action – Combining Work and Family', p.1.

p.186. 'What in the World has the UN got to do with Women?' Labour Party report for the United Nations Fourth World Conference on Women Beijing 1995, June 1995, p.8.

p.187. 'What in the World has the UN got to do with Women?' Labour Party report for the United Nations Fourth World Conference on Women

Beijing 1995, June 1995, introduction by Clare
Short p iii; Equal Opportunities Commission
briefing paper, 'National Agenda for Action –
Combining Work and Family', p.7.

p.190. US National Centre for Health Statistics, the
Harpers Index Book.

p.191. Women's Environmental Network sanitary
protection briefing paper.

p. 192. Greenpeace International. Personal
correspondence, 1995.

p.194. Survey of Disability in Great Britain 1988,
Office of Population Censuses and Surveys.

p.198. Market Opinion and Research Institute
(MORI) survey for Oil of Ulay, July 1995.

p.200. *Cosmopolitan*, 1994 Achievement Awards,
Performing Arts and Overall Winner.

p.203. Shere Hite 'Woman and Love' Survey, 1988.

p.204. Market Opinion and Research Institute
(MORI) survey 'Women in the '90s' June 1995.

p.206. Survey by the Museum of Women's Art,
from information provided by the galleries.

Action!

What if talking, writing postcards and reading them isn't enough? There are women who have organised, lobbied, spoken out and activated! Many women have got together to enjoy each other's company, to raise money for a good cause or to have some time off. If you want to join them or set up your own group, here are some addresses that might help. If you write to a charity or pressure group please send an sae or donation for information.

Co-ordinating/Umbrella Organisations
Women's National Commission
Caxton House, Tothill Street, London SW1H 9NF
Advisory body to the Government.

Wales Assembly of Women
3 Cefn Esgair, Llanbadarn Fawn, Aberystwyth, Wales SY23 3JG

National Alliance of Women's Organisations
PO Box 257, Twickenham, Middlesex TW1 4XG
To bring together widely diverse women's organisations to achieve true equality and justice for all women.

Women's Forum Scotland
c/o 18 Melville Terrace, Stirling FK8 2NQ
Equal opportunities umbrella organisation.

Equal Opportunities Commission
Overseas House, Quay Street, Manchester M3 3HN

National Council of Women of Great Britain (NCW)
36 Danbury Street, London N1 8JU

Campaigning Groups
Rights of Women
52–54 Featherstone Street, London EC1Y 8RT
Informing women of their rights and promoting the interests of women in relation to the law.

Fawcett
5th Floor, 45 Beech St, London EC2Y 8AD
Campaigns for women's equality.

Women Against Fundamentalism
129 Seven Sisters Road, London N7 7QG

WEN – The Women's Environmental Network
Aberdeen Studios, 22 Highbury Grove,
London N5 2EA
Addresses environmental issues that specifically
affect women.

Women's Communications Centre
3–4 Albion Place, London W6 0LT
To advance equality and understanding between
the sexes and to promote women's voices in
public debate.

National Union of Students Women's Campaign
461 Holloway Road, London N7 6LJ

Women for Improved Transport
12 Bartholomew Road, London NW5 2LL

Justice for Women
55 Rathcoole Gardens, London N8 9NE
Set up to campaign against discrimination within
the legal system towards women subjected to
male violence.

Women Against Violence Against Women
52–4 Featherstone Street, London EC1 8YT

Women Against Sexual Harassment (WASH)
312 The Chandlery, 50 Westminster Bridge Road
London SE1 7QY

Childcare/parenting/birthing issues
National Childminding Association
8 Masons Hill, Bromley, Kent BR2 9EY
Campaigns for the resources necessary for a high
quality childminding service.

Working Mothers Association
77 Holloway Road, London N7 8JZ
Provides support for working parents and
information about childcare to employers and
policy makers.

Working for Childcare
77 Holloway Road, London N7 8JZ
National organisation of workplace nurseries.
Promotes the development of quality childcare.

Maternity Alliance
5th Floor, 45 Beech Street, London EC2Y 8AD

AIMS – Association for Improvements in the Maternity Services
40 Kingswood Ave, London NW6 6LS

Employment
New Ways to Work
309 Upper Street, London N1 2TY. Promotes job-sharing and other flexible ways of working.

Opportunity 2000
Business in the Community, 8 Stratton Street, London W1X 5FD
Employer-led campaign to increase quantity and quality of women's participation in the workforce.

Trades Union Congress Equal Rights Department
Great Russell Street, London WC1B 3LS
Can supply a list of affiliated trade unions. Unions help bargain for equal pay, childcare, training, equal opportunities and safer working environments.

Pay Equity Commission
c/o 46 Clonmore Street, London SW1H 5EY

Wages for Housework Campaign
71 Tonbridge Street, London WC1H 9DZ

Health
National Abortion Campaign
The Print House, 18 Ashwin Street, London E8 3DL

Positively Women
5 Sebastian Street, London EC1V OHE

Women's Counselling and Therapy Service Limited
Oxford Chambers, Oxford Place, Leeds LS1 3AX

Women's Health
52–54 Featherstone Street
London EC1Y 8RT

Women's Health Network
National Community Health Resource
57 Charlton Street
London NW1 1HU

Human rights/International Solidarity
Amnesty International
99–119 Rosebery Avenue, London EC1R 4RE

Oxfam
Gender and Development Unit, 34 Banbury Road,
Oxford OX1

Womankind Worldwide
Thettub, 3–4 Albion Pl., London W6 0LT
Dedicated towards positive change in the lives of
women throughout the developing world.

*United Nations Division for the Advancement of
Women*
Room E-1273/5041, Vienna International Centre,
PO Box 500, A-1400 Vienna, Austria

Women of Colour/ethnic minority
Akina Mama Wa Afrika
Wesley House, 4 Wildcourt, London WC2B 5AU

Asian Young Women's Project
8 Manor Gardens, London N7 6LZ
Bangladesh Women's Association
91 Highbury Hill
London N5 1SX

Chinese Association of Women's Groups
680 Commercial Road, Sailors Place,
London E14 7HA

League of Jewish Women
Woburn House, Upper Woburn Place
London WC1H OEP

London Irish Women's Centre
59 Stoke Newington Church Street,
London N16 OAR

Muslim Women's Welfare Association
School Annexe, Bickley Road, London E10 7HL

Southall Black Sisters
52 Norwood Road, Southall, Middlesex UB2 4DW

Union of Turkish Women in Britain
110 Clarence Road, London E5 8JA

Politics
The 300 Group
19 Borough High Street, London SE1 9SE
All-party campaign for women in politics and
public life.

Women into Public Life
110 Riverview Gardens, London SW13 9RA
Encourages/advises women to aspire to public
office.

Conservative National Women's Committee
32 Smith Square, London SW1P 3HH

Emily's List UK
PO Box 708, London SW10 ODH

Labour Women
150 Walworth Road, London SE17 1JT

Women in Local Government Working Group
c/o Viv Bates
Sandwell Metropolitan Borough Council, West
Midlands

Women Liberal Democrats
4 Cowley Street, London SW1P 3NB

Women's Party
Box 29 Sisterwrite, 190 Upper Street, London N1

Women's Networks and Membership Organisations
Associated Country Women of the World
Vincent House, Vincent Square, London SW1P 2NB

Women's Institutes
(National Federation of)
104 New Kings Road, London SW6 4LY

Townswomen's Guilds
Chamber of Commerce House
75 Harbourne Road, Edgbaston,
Birmingham B15 3DA

National Women's Register (NWR)
(was National Housewive's Register)
9 Bank Plain, Norwich, Norfolk NR2 4SL

City Women's Network
PO Box 353, Uxbridge UB10 0UN

Mothers' Union
24 Tufton Street, London SW1P 3RB

Soroptimists International
7 Trentdale Road, Carlton, Notts. NG4 1BU

National Association of Widows
54–57 Allison Street, Digbeth, Birmingham B5 5TH

British Association of Women Entrepreneurs
33 Caithness Road, London W14 0JA

Business and Professional Women's Federation
23 Ansdell Street, London W8 5BN

European Network of Women (UK)
2 Wesley Street, Castleford, West Yorks WF10 1AE

Women in Film and Television
11–15 Betterton Street, London WC2H 9BP

Women and Manual Trades
52–54 Featherstone Street, London EC1Y 8RT